The After-School Lives of Children

Alone and With Others
While Parents Work

The After-School Lives of Children

Alone and With Others While Parents Work

Deborah Belle

Boston University

LEA LAWRENCE ERLBAUM ASSOCIATES, PUBLISHERS
1999 Mahwah, New Jersey London

Some material in this book appeared originally in D. Belle (1997). Varieties of self-care: A qualitative look at children's experiences in the after-school hours. *Merrill-Palmer Quarterly,* 43, no. 3, 478–496 and in D. Belle, S, Norell, & A. Lewis (1997). Becoming supervised: Children's transitions from adult-care to self-care in the afterschool hours. In I. Gotlib & B. Wheaton (Eds.) *Stress and adversity over the life course: Trajectories and turning point* (pp. 159–178). Cambridge: Cambridge University Press.

Lawrence Erlbaum Associate, Inc., Publishers
10 Industrial Avenue
Mahwah, NJ 07430

Cover design by Kathryn Houghtaling Lacey
Cover illustration by Charlotte Andry Gibbs

Library of Congress Cataloging-in-Publication Data

Belle, Deborah
The after-school lives of children : alone and with others while parents work / Deborah Belle
p. cm.
Includes bibliographical references and index.
ISBN 0-8058-2325-5 (hc. : alk. paper)
1. Latchkey children--United States--Social condition. 2. Children of working parents--United States--Social condition.
I. Title.
HQ777.65.845 1999
305.23'0973--dc21 99-17931
CIP

Books published by Lawrence Erlbaum Associates are printed on acid-free paper, and their bindings are chosen for strength and durability

Printed in the Untied States of America
10 9 8 7 6 5 4 3 2

For Steve

Contents

Preface

At least 3.5 million school-age children in the United States regularly spend after-school time unsupervised by adults or older teenagers, and most discussions of this reality begin with the assumption that lack of supervision is problematic for children. Yet empirical research has produced unexpected findings. Some studies report problems for unsupervised children; others find no differences between supervised and unsupervised children; and credible studies have reported poorer outcomes for children who spend after-school time with older siblings, babysitters, after-school teachers, and their own mothers, than for children who spend after-school time on their own.

Most studies of unsupervised or *latchkey* children have ignored the tremendous variation among self-care arrangements, and very few studies have followed children from year to year to discover the significance to children of changes in after-school arrangements over time. Few studies attend to the viewpoints of both parents and children, and there are virtually no studies that give voice to either parents or children grappling with after-school issues. Most studies have looked for statistical associations between aspects of children's after-school arrangements and indicators of their well-being. Little research has examined the processes by which after-school arrangements might affect children.

I began the research reported here to explore the nature of children's lives after school when parents are away at work. The study was limited to families in which parents were employed full time and in which there was at least one child in elementary school at the start of the study. The research families included single-parent, two-parent, and joint-custody families from a wide range of socioeconomic and ethnic backgrounds. Over a 4-year period, mothers, fathers, and their children were interviewed annually about the child's after-school arrangements. Speaking individually and privately to interviewers, parents and children told their own stories about after-school dilemmas and after-school experiences.

Drawing on the stories these parents and children told, and often on their actual words, this book emphasizes the wide variety of children's after-school arrangements, children's movement over time in and out of different arrangements, and the importance to children of multiple facets of their after-school arrangements, not simply the presence or absence of an adult caretaker. I also emphasize that children are not randomly assigned to after-school arrangements. Rather, parents and children struggle to reach optimal solutions to what are often difficult child-care dilemmas. To understand these dilemmas and the diverse strategies that families adopt, one must attend to the individual situations of children as family members understand them.

The historic trends that have led so many children in late 20th-century America to be unsupervised after school show no signs of reversing. Mothers as well as fathers are in the paid labor force to stay. Even grandmothers, who once provided a ready source of care for children, are now likely to be employed themselves. Divorce and the birth of children to unmarried parents continue to produce large numbers of single-parent households. The low wages paid to many workers, particularly those without advanced education, often require that they work even more than one full-time job simply to make ends meet. As we adjust to the new realities of family life in the United States, it becomes clear that creative new practices and policies are needed to help families handle the awkward time of day when children have returned from school but parents are still at work.

I hope this book contributes to the development of such policies and practices by illuminating the difficulties families face and their consequences for children. *The After-School Lives of Children* is written for psychologists, sociologists, and other social scientists who study families, maternal employment, child care, or child development, and for parents, educators, community leaders, and public policymakers concerned about the well-being of children whose parents are employed.

ACKNOWLEDGMENTS

For many stimulating conversations about this project I am grateful to my colleagues in the William T. Grant Foundation's Faculty Scholars Program and its Consortium for Research on Stress Processes, as well as to my community of sister-fellows at the Bunting Institute at Radcliffe College. Financial support from the William T. Grant Foundation and the National institute of Mental Health was crucial to this project, as was the opportunity to spend a sabbatical year at the Bunting Institute as an Evelyn Green Davis fellow. I am particularly grateful to Robert Haggerty and Beatrix Hamburg of the Grant Foundation and to Florence Ladd of the Bunting Institute for their faith in me and in this project.

I was very fortunate in the interviewers who joined me in this effort: Liz April, Debra Bolter, Cliff Bromberg, Robin Burr, Joanne Greenfield, Peg Heffernan, Jordan Lee, Lisa Livshin, Sukie Magraw, Margaret Miller, Beth Pinals, Chris Ratiner, Tracey Rogers, Jacqueline Schonholtz, Oria Shadmon, K. C. Turnbull, Scott Watanabe, and Ann Woodbury.

After the interviews were completed Robin Burr, Michelle Caya, Julia Chou, Lisa Hunter, Anne Noonan, and Maureen Reese helped me to think about each child and each family. Sara Norell, Anthony Lewis, and Denise Hines worked on the table that appears in chapter 2. Stephanie Stein organized a great deal of material on the families in the study. Diane Pfaelzer and Tzu-Yi Chen helped put together information on sibling relationships.

Robin Burr was part of this project from before its beginning until after its end. Her insights into families shaped this study in important ways, while her unwavering enthusiasm for this work sustained me. Michelle Seligson alerted me to crucial issues in the provision of after-school care. Jackie James suggested important interview questions for parents about their own childhood experiences with employed parents and unsupervised time. I am also grateful for the thoughtful criticism and support of David Riley and Judith Amsel.

To the research families I owe a tremendous debt. Their willingness to discuss the often charged issues of after-school time, and their ability to convey the complexities of their lives made this study possible.

I am also deeply grateful to my husband, Steve, and to my sons, Joshua and Daniel, for making my life so rich and so meaningful while I worked on this book.

—Deborah Belle

1

Introduction

When the school day ends, 7-year-old Meiguei Chen takes the school bus and heads to the children's room of her town's public library, where she remains until her mother picks her up 3 hours later. Although the librarians are aware of Meiguei's presence and unofficially keep an eye on her, they have no formal responsibility for her. She spends most of her time at the library reading.

Jason Lehman has a 45-minute bus ride to his after-school program, which he has been attending since he was in second grade. He is now an 11-year-old fifth grader. At his after-school program, Jason can choose from sports activities, cooking, arts and crafts, videos, and games. Jason attends the program on most of the days that he spends each week with his father. On the days Jason lives with his mother, he can choose between going to the after-school program, staying home alone or with a friend, visiting the town library, or going to his father's store.

Ten-year-old Dominique Nelson always does her homework right away when she comes home from school. She has several hours to herself each afternoon before she picks up her 3-year-old sister at the nearby child-care center and walks her home. Dominique then does housework, plays, watches television, and cares for her sister until their mother returns home from work around 8 p.m.

Children of employed parents spend their after-school time in diverse ways. Some are supervised by adults, others are not, and some children have arrangements that are not easily characterized. Some children spend many hours alone after school, while others are generally in the company of siblings, peers, or adults. Many spend time in their own homes, others at libraries, after-school programs, parks, or the homes of friends. Some have considerable freedom to travel around their communities after school, while others are fixed within a narrow radius, perhaps the walls of their own apartments. Child care and housework are major responsibilities for some children. Others refine skills in music, sports, or languages. Some children are physically active, while others spend much of their time in quiet reading or contemplation of the television set.

Perhaps what is most striking is that families have arrived at so many different responses to this awkward time of day, when children have been dismissed from school and parents are at work. Each family invents its own solution to the dilemmas posed by after-school time. Each child experiences the after-school hours differently.

Although each family crafts its own solution to the problem of after-school hours, all families do so within constraints set by larger social forces: the nature of the U.S. economy, the demands of the parental workplace, the schedule of the school day, the availability of affordable child-care options, and public norms and rules about the care of children.

THE DEMANDS ON PARENTS

It is hardly surprising that many U.S. children no longer have a parent at home to supervise their after-school activities. Maternal employment, like paternal employment, is normative. In 1990, 75% of mothers with school-aged children were employed, most of them full time (U.S. Dept. of Labor, 1991). In fact, moonlighting, or holding multiple jobs, increased by 500% among women between 1970 and 1989 (Coontz, 1992). Fuchs (1988) calculated that between 1960 and 1986 the time parents had to spend with children fell 10 hours per week for Whites and 12 hours for Blacks.

Parents increasingly need to work long hours to maintain a middle-class lifestyle and simply to stay out of poverty. The minimum wage was lower in

1995, adjusting for inflation, than it was in 1950, and the average hourly wage in 1995 was lower than it was in 1968 (Folbre & the Center for Popular Economics, 1995). Half the new jobs created in the 1980s paid a wage lower than the poverty figure for a family of four (Coontz, 1992), and more than one third of all two-parent families in 1998 would be poor if both parents did not work (Coontz, 1992). In 1989, almost 8 out of 10 home buyers came from two-income households (Coontz, 1992). Close to half of all children will spend time in a single-parent household, usually one headed by a mother, before they are 18 (Furstenberg, 1994), and neither government payments to such families nor the economic assistance provided by absent fathers tends to support female-headed families above the poverty level. Among the 165 low-wage working mothers Edin and Lein (1997) interviewed, none could completely support their families on income from their full-time jobs, and three fifths of these women worked overtime at their main jobs or took a second job to make ends meet.

In international perspective, U.S. parents bear an unusually heavy burden of combined work and family responsibilities (Scarr, 1991), with few supportive or responsive institutions to make the burden lighter. In most industrialized countries, taxes subsidize parental leaves and child care. Scarr noted that European parents provide only between 6% and 15% of the cost of their children's care, Canadian parents provide 60% to 70%, but in the United States, parents provide more than 90% of the child-care costs. The operating cost of U.S. child-care centers has remained about the same since the 1970s, but public funds have supported a smaller and smaller proportion of this cost, leaving parents to pay more and more (Whitebook, Howes, & Phillips, 1990, cited in Zigler & Finn-Stevenson, 1995). In many societies, relatives take a larger share in child- rearing and income production, easing stress on parents and providing a larger network of support for children as well. U.S. society is highly individualistic, and many families today truly sink or swim on their own.

HISTORICAL AND CROSS-CULTURAL PERSPECTIVES

Contemporary trends in maternal employment are sometimes seen as representing a profound break with the rest of human history. Yet, as historians and anthropologists remind us, mothers have always engaged in productive labor as well as in the reproductive labor of bearing and caring for children. Among hunting-and-gathering groups, women gather edible roots and berries for their families and bring home firewood and water. Among farm families, women tend to the poultry, the dairy, the preserving of foods. During Colonial times, women ran inns, shops, and other businesses, and produced clothing, furniture, candles, and other necessities in their own homes (Bernard, 1981). As Bernard noted, John Adams depended on his wife, Abigail, to manage the family estate, allowing John to attend to the business of nation-building. In 19th-century America, many women added to the family income by taking in lodgers and boarders, doing laundry, or doing piecework sewing at home. Throughout U.S. history, poor women, immigrant women, and African-American women have often had to work, even at times when they were responsible for children. Historically and cross-culturally, it has been unusual for any human group to dispense with the productive labor of women, including mothers.

Nor, from an historical or cross-cultural perspective, is children's freedom from adult supervision a great novelty. In 19th-century U.S. cities, children spent much of their time on the streets with other children, unsupervised by adults (Hareven, 1989). In immigrant families, children of 8 or 10 took care of younger siblings while their parents worked (Hareven, 1989). In many non-Western cultures, young children are supervised more often by siblings than by parents (Weisner & Gallimore, 1977), and are required to exhibit far more independence and responsibility than are generally expected from U.S. children today (Whiting & Whiting, 1975). Yet the similarities between sibling caretaking in non-Western cultures and in our own should not be overdrawn. In non-Western cultures sibling caretakers are typically within earshot or easy reach of responsible adults, which may not be the case in U.S. communities. The homestead or village settlement patterns of many other cultures do not foster the isolation of child caretaker and charge that can be found in many city apartments today. Nor, in such homesteads or villages, does social stigma surround the use of sibling caretakers.

In the recent past, Silverstein and Krate (1975) found that the Harlem children they studied who were nominally supervised by a relative or neighbor still spent more of their out-of-school time in the streets with peers. Similarly, Keller (1963) reported that school-age slum children showed little sustained contact with adults, and Bronfenbrenner (1967) argued that such a pattern characterizes school-age children across class and ethnic lines. Children we think of as supervised may be those who have access to parents and are accessible to parents, without being constantly within the parent's visual field.

In comparison to the children in many nonindustrialized nations and to children in an earlier America, U.S. children in the late 20th century tend to spend strikingly little time contributing to the household economy (Wenger, 1989; Whiting & Edwards, 1988; Zelizer, 1985). And when U.S. children are asked to make such contributions, they tend to react differently than do children for whom household work is understood as a shared responsibility. According to Wenger (1989), the cultural meanings of children's household tasks are evident from the responses children make when such tasks are assigned. "Many American children see the assignment of chores as the product of parental personal prerogative. A chore, from this perspective, is a concession—of one individual to another—to be negotiated around and, possibly, resisted" (p. 92). In contrast, the Giriama children in rural Kenya whom Wenger studied "participate, at some level, in the shared cultural understanding that the tasks requested are necessary to the well-being of household members, and thus they recognize that task assignment has a wider legitimacy than personal prerogative"(p. 92).

Wenger noted that the young children she observed take great pleasure in being asked to perform small errands and experience great satisfaction at completing their tasks. In describing social life among the Abaluyia, another Bantu-speaking group in rural Kenya, Weisner (1989) reported similar themes. Assigning children tasks, asking for their help, and involving them in work "all seem comforting and supportive for Abaluyia children" (p. 79). Weisner noted that such "shared-management" practices "emphasize interdependence more than autonomy" (p. 78) and prepare children for an adulthood of continued affiliation and collaboration with kin. Giriama adults believe that without such training in responsibility and mutuality, children will arrive at adulthood "with few prospects and without the respect of the community" (Wenger, 1989, p. 93).

There may, paradoxically, be danger in providing for children an environment that demands too little of them. Elder (1974) argued that U.S. society deprives young people of "challenging situations in which they could make valuable contributions to family and community welfare" (p. 292). Children whose families faced economic deprivation during the Great Depression frequently took on more responsibilities within the household and paying jobs outside the household. In addition, the economic stress they experienced heightened their appreciation of their parents' efforts to provide the goods and services they had earlier taken for granted.

> Economic scarcity brought out the reciprocal aspects of consumption which entail obligations to others. Especially in middle-class families, deprivation generally changed one-sided dependency regimes, in which parents indulged their offspring's desires, to an arrangement where children were expected to demonstrate more self-reliance in caring for themselves and family needs. (Elder, 1974, p. 66)

Working together for the common good of the family was often a meaningful experience that brought family members closer.

In his classic study of the Great Depression, Elder (1974) found that men who as children had experienced drastic family income loss actually achieved higher occupational status, on average, than those men whose families had not experienced such severe deprivation. Elder showed that the positive impact of economic deprivation was mediated by the earlier attainment of well-defined vocational interests in the boys from economically deprived families. Similarly, in their longitudinal study of vulnerability and resilience, Werner and Smith (1982) found that for children growing up in difficult life situations, acts of "required helpfulness," such as performing household chores, caring for siblings, and working for pay to help support the family, were associated with resilience.

Whiting and Whiting (1975) argued that the degree to which children are expected to be responsible and independent from adults is predicted by the extent of women's work loads. In line with this principle, observers have noted parents' higher demands for such responsibility and independence from children in single-parent households (Weiss, 1979), African-American households (McLoyd, 1993), economically deprived households during the Great Depression (Elder, 1974), and low-income households where mothers are overburdened (Jeffers, 1967; Silverstein & Krate, 1975; Zelkowitz, 1982b). As U.S. women increasingly take on paid labor in addition to child-care and household maintenance responsibilities, children will probably experience even greater demands for independence and responsibility.

The physical separation of women's productive labor from their homes, where they could also keep an eye on children, has had a great impact on family life. It was the industrial revolution that severed work from home, and although children and unmarried women were among the first workers to "man" the factories of this revolution, in the 20th century it has more often been men who left home for work. In the late 20th century, the inexorable logic of this revolution has pulled women as well away from their homes. Although we have had more than a century to accustom ourselves to fathers' removal from the home, we are not so accustomed to mothers' absence.

Certainly the schools behave as if mothers remained at home to attend to children. The U.S. public school day is substantially shorter than the full-time work day and shorter than the school day in many other nations of the world. The school year is also interrupted by frequent holidays, early release days, and closings for inclement weather, and then concluded with a lengthy summer vacation, all of which vastly exceeds the vacation allotments of most employed parents. Nor are extended day or after-school programs available in many communities or to many children who need them.

Ironically, we owe the shape of our school calendar to earlier efforts to make the child's school day compatible with the needs of working families. As Googins (1991) pointed out, "Schools were originally structured around the needs of the workplace" (p. 255). But in an earlier, rural America, that workplace was the farm. The school day began at 9 a.m. so that children could complete their morning chores before school, and school closed for July and August so that children could help out on the family farm when their efforts were most needed. America long ago ceased to be an agrarian society, but the school calender has not evolved in concert with the country.

Throughout much of the 20th century, many Americans have believed strongly that children should be cared for during the day by their own mothers. This belief led many who thought they were supporting the well-being of children and mothers to fight against the establishment of child-care centers that would have allowed women to combine employment with maternal responsibilities. In 1905, there were only 206 day nurseries in the entire country (Gordon, 1994). Lacking day care, mothers who needed to work were often forced to send their children to orphanages or foster families. In the early part of the century, most children in orphanages had living parents, frequently widowed mothers who could not support them (Gordon, 1994).

Yet U.S. history also includes instances in which day care (including after-school and evening care) was provided for the children of working women, allowing mothers to support their children economically while still residing with them. One grim example is that group nurseries were sometimes established on slave plantations to care for the children of slave women who labored in the fields (Youcha, 1995). Dame schools in colonial New England and infant schools during the 1820s and 1830s provided instruction and supervision even to very young children. During World War II, child-care centers were established under the Lanham Act to provide care for the children of women working in the war effort. Some centers provided before-school, after-school, and even round-the-clock care in response to women's work schedules. Yet at the conclusion of the war, most of these centers were rapidly phased out, and the precedent they had set in providing government-assisted child care for the children of employed mothers was largely forgotten (Youcha, 1995).

In many U.S. families in the late 20th century, no parent returns home from work until hours after the school day has ended. Some children attend formal after-school programs during these hours or return home to a grandparent or other adult caretaker. During the elementary school years, however, children often begin to spend time after school on their own. Hofferth, Brayfield, Deich, and Holcomb (1991) reported that in 1990 some 3.5 million school-age children in the United States regularly spent time unsupervised by adults or older teenagers, a figure almost double that derived from a similar survey conducted in 1984 (Cain & Hofferth, 1989).

THINKING ABOUT SUPERVISION AND LACK OF SUPERVISION

During World War II, Zucker (1944) saw maladjustment and delinquency looming for *latchkey* children whose mothers sought wartime employment. "The house key tied around the neck is the symbol of cold meals, of a child neglected and shorn of the security of a mother's love and affection" (p. 43). More recently, a survey found that school teachers and parents attribute poor school performance primarily to children's lack of care and supervision in the after-school hours (Harris, Louis, & Associates, Inc., 1987, cited in Seligson, 1991). As Medrich, Roizen, Rubin, and Buckley (1982) observed:

> Many feel that children this age should be within safe distance, if not under the actual supervision of adults most of the time. They should move each day from one sphere of adult influence, the school, to another, the home, as rapidly as possible. When this ideal goes unrealized, as it often does, a "problem" is readily inferred, either in parenting or in the social provision of child care. (p. 63)

The success of the *Home Alone* films testifies to our horrified fascination with the idea of children on their own, as does public interest in the cases of parents who leave their children alone while they vacation far away. Newspaper discussions of the films and the court cases frequently allude to the more commonplace experiences of children on their own after school, drawing a connection and a moral, a parable for our time.

Today's parents are often reluctant to allow their children to range widely. To many parents, the world outside is full of dangers, and prudence dictates that children should be kept close to home or under the watchful eye of responsible adults (Knight, 1997). Children's freedom to explore is often limited for fear of sexual assault and abduction, injuries, and even natural hazards such as Lyme disease. The fear of litigation often keeps nonparental caretakers from allowing children to engage in risky behaviors such as climbing trees or even from simply venturing out of sight.

As Knight (1997) pointed out, the dangers parents fear, especially abduction and sexual assault by strangers, are rare, and, in many towns and suburbs are no more common than they were a generation ago. Yet, tragic assaults on children in any part of the country receive avid media attention throughout the entire country, creating a perception of danger that affects parents, no matter what the reality.

A widely cited Carnegie Foundation report (Carnegie Corporation of New York, 1992) states that adolescents are most likely to engage in sexual intercourse during unsupervised time after school. However, the reference cited to support this assertion (Zelnik & Kantner, 1977) contains no data on the time of day at which adolescents are most likely to engage in sexual intercourse or on the association between adult supervision and adolescent sexual activity. The linking of risky and disapproved activities to unsupervised after-school time is apparently so strong, however, that this assertion has been widely repeated and believed without further scrutiny.

Many observers are quick to connect inadequate supervision of children to maternal employment. In arguing for a connection between improper parental supervision and teenage pregnancies, C. Williams (1991), for instance, began by discussing the lack of adequate after-school activities and recreational programs for young people whose parents work long hours. The stories she related about lack of supervision, however, generally indict maternal inattention that is unrelated to employment. She wrote of one mother who got involved with a cocaine addict and left her young daughter alone for 3 or 4 days at a time, another who often went out partying in the late evening and did not return home until the next morning. Yet another of the adolescents Williams described ran away from home at 13 to escape her mother's strict supervision. These case studies demonstrate the importance of sustained and sensitive parental attention, but hardly indict maternal employment as the culprit in producing parental inattention.

DEVELOPMENTAL PERSPECTIVES

Although unsupervised children clearly violate the sensibilities of many observers, developmental theory suggests a more complex view. During middle childhood (the years from ages 6 to 12) and early adolescence (ages 10 to 14), children appear to benefit from appropriate opportunities for independence and responsibility, particularly in the context of supportive relationships with parents and other adults. As Hoffman (1979) argued, school-age children still need "love, guidance, a boost in confidence, a home base," but they also need "independence, a chance to cope on their own, an opportunity to develop a sense of responsibility and a feeling of competence" (p. 862). Bryant (1994, p. 23) maintained that children as well as adults need experiences of independence, privacy, and solitude.

According to Bryant (1989), the need for autonomy is lifelong. Infants benefit when they can explore their own environments and exert some control over the course of interactions with their caretakers. Children benefit when they can choose to be alone as well as in the company of others. Adolescents benefit when granted some autonomy in decision making. Workers benefit when allowed some control over the timing and content of work tasks, and older adults benefit when they can choose activities they personally find rewarding.

In her own empirical study of middle childhood, Bryant (1989) showed that children benefit when they experience autonomy from adults as well as support and supervision from them. She contrasted children who presumably receive considerable adult attention but fewer opportunities for independent exploration (children whose mothers are not employed; children in small families), with children who presumably experience the opposite pattern (children with mothers employed full time; children in large families). Children whose mothers were employed full time appeared to benefit from adult-supervised activities outside of school, whereas children whose mothers were not employed did not benefit from such activities, but seemed to benefit from greater informal peer involvement away from adults. Similarly, children in small families appeared to benefit from privacy, autonomy, and independence experiences away from adults, whereas children in larger families benefited more from additional involvements by parents and grandparents (Bryant, 1985, 1989).

Eccles et al. (1993) noted that the early adolescent years are frequently marked by family conflict over issues related to autonomy and control. Disagreements between parents and children about authority relationships in the family reach their peak in the early adolescent years. Eccles et al. also found that excessive parental control is associated with emotional, motivational, and conduct problems in young people. Bryant (1994) argued that parental concern with protecting children from physical danger "can blind adults to the value that privacy and other forms of autonomy have for well-being and growth" (p. 23). Richards and Duckett (1991) suggested that with adolescents, parents need to be "available but not omnipresent" (p. 87).

Developmentally, middle childhood is a time in which parents continue to exercise supervisory control over their children, but in which children "begin to exercise moment-to-moment self-regulation" (Maccoby, 1984, p. 191). This delicate process of "co-regulation" only succeeds, according to Maccoby, when parents effectively aid their children when they are together; monitor, guide, and support their children when they are separated; and strengthen their children's abilities to keep their own behavior within safe limits and to know when they should turn to parents. Communication from parent to child and from child to parent is essential so that parents can aid their children when necessary.

The premature granting of independence can be problematic, as can independence without parental care. Children's risk of serious injury in the home rises when they do not have an adult caregiver (Peterson, 1989). Antisocial and risky behaviors such as drug use are more common in young people when their parents do not monitor their behavior, even at a distance, and when parents are uninvolved and uninformed about their children's lives (Feiring & Lewis, 1991; Maccoby, 1984; Sampson, 1992).

CONTEMPORARY QUESTIONS

Although historians and anthropologists have deepened our understanding of the origins of the situation we face in the late 1990s, parents and community leaders urgently need information about the immediate needs of children. What are we to make of the nature of our children's lives today, when parents generally cannot be with their children after the school day ends? How should we respond? Do children unsupervised in the after-school hours experience beneficial chances "to cope on their own," or malign experiences of premature independence? Is lack of supervision a danger to children, or simply an inevitable marker on the pathway toward adult independence? Thinking about children's lives after school inevitably leads us to examine the nature of childhood and the compact between parents and children. We are led to reflect on the roles of mothers and fathers, and on the place of the larger society in supporting families.

In the following chapter, I critically review the empirical research on lack of adult supervision as a risk factor for children, pointing both to the methodological limitations of the studies and to their underlying assumptions about the role of adult supervision in children's lives.

In subsequent chapters, I discuss the quandaries parents face in trying to find suitable after-school arrangements for their children, the forces that lead children into particular kinds of after-school arrangements over time, the challenges children face in the after-school hours when parents are at work, the support children derive from the important people in their lives, and the significance for children and for families of the after-school arrangements that are made. These chapters rely on an intensive study, described more fully in chapter 3, of 53 children and their employed parents, who were interviewed annually for 4 years about the children's after-school arrangements and their emotional, behavioral, and academic well-being. The book concludes with a final chapter in which I discuss the implications of what has been learned for family decision making, public policies, and future research.

2

Do School-Age Children Need Adult Supervision?

Although Zucker (1944) was the first to publish concerns about unsupervised children, the earliest systematic research to assess the well-being of such children is probably Woods' (1972) study, "The Unsupervised Child of the Working Mother." This study, although often summarized as simply demonstrating the dangers of lack of supervision, actually encapsulates many of the fascinating complexities that continue to characterize more recent work.

Woods administered academic and personality tests to 108 low-income and predominantly Black fifth graders whose mothers were employed at least part time, obtained teacher ratings of these children, interviewed 38 of the employed mothers, and combed school, hospital, and police records to learn more about the children. Relying on children's reports of their supervision status, Woods found that unsupervised girls, but not unsupervised boys, performed more poorly on academic tasks than their supervised peers.

However, her detailed interviews with mothers produced a very different picture. The children whose school and social adjustment was the best and whose IQ scores were the highest had mothers who were employed full time and absent from home before school, during the lunch hour, and after school. Furthermore, those children who had complete responsibility for their siblings and very extensive household responsibilities excelled in many achievement and intelligence tests. These results surprised Woods and led her to revise her understanding of household responsibilities for children (Woods, 1972).

> Where there is genuine need for the child's help around the house, as is almost certainly true in lower-class families with working mothers, the "chores" he does may have the same meaning in terms of character building ascribed to the nineteenth century farm boys' chores. If this were true one might expect the posture of responsibility and commitment to doing one's best to carry over into school work. Alternatively the explanation may be much simpler: Perhaps mothers were aware of the high level of intelligence and achievement of those they assigned excessive responsibility to. (p. 21)

Woods also found that children who enjoyed positive relationships with their mothers and those whose mothers were happy to be employed tended to excel at school. Unfortunately, Woods did not grapple directly with the seemingly contradictory themes in her work—the negative correlates of unsupervised time, but the positive correlates of full-time maternal employment, heavy household responsibilities, and sibling caretaking, which would seem to imply a lack of adult supervision.

RESEARCH METHODS

Since this pioneering effort there have been fewer studies of unsupervised children than might have been expected, given the extent of popular concern with this issue. Published empirical studies are shown in Table 2.1. As can be seen, the methodological characteristics of these studies limit our ability to draw clear conclusions from the research.

Determining Causality

Many of the studies use cross-sectional designs, which makes it impossible to be certain that the presumed outcome variables have not led to the

TABLE 2.1
Empirical Studies Contrasting the Well-Being of Self-Care and Supervised Children

Study	*Time Frame*	*Questionnaires/ Interviews*	*Sample*	*Excludes Nonemployed Parents?*	*Definition of Self-Care*	*Who Describes Arrangement?*	*Reliability of Description Assessed?*	*Variables*	*Negative Consequences for Self-Care Children Compared to Supervised Children?*
Woods (1972)	Cross-sectional	Questionnaires and interviews	108 fifth graders; Black, urban, low income	Yes	Unsupervised by an adult > 18 years old	Child and mother	Yes	Personal and social adjustment, intelligence, school achievement, health, family relationships, school behavior, community behaviors	Yes, for girls only
Long and Long (1982)	Cross-sectional	Semi-structured interviews	85 Grade 1–6 children; Black, urban	No	Alone routinely during after-school hours with or without siblings	Child	No	Self-help skills, personal responsi-bility, fear development (coping,	Yes

(continues)

TABLE 2.1 *(continued)*

Study	*Time Frame*	*Question-naires/ Interviews*	*Sample*	*Excludes Nonemployed Parents?*	*Definition of Self-Care*	*Who Describes Arrangement?*	*Reliability of Description Assessed?*	*Variables*	*Negative Consequences for Self-Care Children Compared to Supervised Children?*
								nightmares, expressed fears), family relationships, and socializing play	
Galambos and Garbarino (1985)	Cross-sectional	Questionnaires and interviews	39 fifth graders & 38 Seventh graders; White; rural; lower middle class	Yes	Alone without adult supervision before or after school	Parents	No	School adjustment, classroom orientation, fear of outdoors, academic achievement	No
Rodman, Pratto, and Nelson (1985)	Cross-sectional	Questionnaires and interviews	52 fourth graders, 44 seventh graders; Racially and socioeconomically diverse	No	Either alone after school or with younger sibling	Child	No	Self-esteem, locus of control, social adjustment, interpersonal relations	No

Toeinniessen, Little, and Rosen (1985)	Cross-sectional	Questionnaires	38 sixth graders; middle class; suburban	No	Without adult supervision for part of each school day, child typically returns from school to an empty house	Parents	No	Five most/least experienced feelings	Yes
L. Steinberg (1986)	Cross-sectional	Questionnaires	865 Fifth–ninth graders; racially and socioeconomically diverse	No	Unsupervised or with a younger sibling or peers after school in various settings	Child	No	Susceptibility to peer pressure	Yes, only for those away from home and without adult monitoring
Vandell and Corasaniti (1988)	Cross-sectional	Questionnaires	150 third graders; White, predominantly middle class	No	At home without adult supervision	Parents	No	Standardized test scores, academic grades, conduct grades, classroom sociometric ratings, work/study	No

(continues)

TABLE 2.1 *(continued)*

Study	*Time Frame*	*Questionnaires/ Interviews*	*Sample*	*Excludes Nonemployed Parents?*	*Definition of Self-Care*	*Who Describes Arrangement?*	*Reliability of Description Assessed?*	*Variables*	*Negative Consequences for Self-Care Children Compared to Supervised Children?*
								skills, emotional well-being, adult–child relationships, self-competence	
Diamond, Kataria, and Messer (1989)	Cross-sectional	Questionnaires	44 fifth & sixth graders; rural	No	Left to care for oneself after school	Child	Yes	Academic achievement, behavior problems, school adjustment	Yes
Lovko and Ullman (1989)	Cross-sectional	Questionnaires	116 grade 3–5 students; predominantly White, middle class	No	Child regularly spends at least 30 minutes per week without direct super-	Parents	No	Anxiety, self-perceived social ability, behavior problems	No

					vision of someone in the seventh grade or older				
Messer, Wuensch, and Diamond (1989)	Retrospective	Questionnaires	188 college students; predominantly White	No	Unsupervised by an adult after school during elementary or middle school years	Student	No	Academic aptitude, personality	No
Richardson et al. (1989)	Cross-sectional	Questionnaires	4,932 eighth graders; socioeconomically and racially diverse	No	Caring for self during out-of-school hours	Child	Yes	Substance use (cigarettes, marijuana, alcohol)	Yes
Dwyer et al. (1990)	Cross-sectional	Questionnaires	4,852 eighth graders; socioeconomically and racially diverse; urban	No	Care of self at least one afternoon or evening per week	Child	Yes	Self-report of grades, substance use (cigarettes, marijuana, alcohol), truancy, risk-taking, peer influences, anger, stress,	Yes

(continues)

TABLE 2.1 *(continued)*

Study	*Time Frame*	*Question-naires/ Interviews*	*Sample*	*Excludes Nonemployed Parents?*	*Definition of Self-Care*	*Who Describes Arrangement?*	*Reliability of Description Assessed?*	*Variables*	*Negative Consequences for Self-Care Children Compared to Supervised Children?*
								fear of being alone, family conflict	
Galambos and Maggs (1991b)	Longitudinal	Questionnaires	112 sixth graders; suburban	Yes	Regularly cares for oneself after school	Child	No	Peer experiences, self-image, parent–child relationships	Yes, only for girls away from home
Vandell and Ramanan (1991)	Cross-sectional	Questionnaires	390 grade 3–5 students; low-income, urban, ethnically diverse	No	Care for self after school or by a sibling less than 15 years old	Mother	No	Cognitive ability, self-perception, behavior problems	Yes, but not when family income and emotional support are controlled
Woodard and Fine (1991)	Retrospective	Questionnaires	248 college students; White, middle/upper socioeconomic status	No	Caring for self or with younger siblings regularly during out-	Student	No	Cognitive adjustment, emotional adjustment, and personality	No

					of-school hours			development	
Berman, Winkleby, Chesterman, and Boyce (1992)	Cross-sectional	Questionnaires	297 fourth and sixth graders; ethnically and racially diverse	No	Without adult supervision after school on more than 3 days a week	Child	Yes	Self-esteem	No
Quay (1992)	Cross-sectional	Questionnaires	582 kinder-gartners – fourth graders; socioeco-nomically diverse	No	Child usually goes to his or her home after school without a parent present	Child	No	Loneliness	Yes, in comparison to those children whose mothers were home with them. Comparisons with children in other supervised settings (e.g., with babysitter) were not significant.
Ross, Saaverdra, Shur, Winters, and	Longitudinal	Questionnaires	888 kinder-gartners – sixth graders;	No	Spend at least some time at home after school	Parent	No	Academic performance, adaptive & maladaptive	No

(continues)

TABLE 2.1 *(continued)*

Study	*Time Frame*	*Question-naires/ Interviews*	*Sample*	*Excludes Nonemployed Parents?*	*Definition of Self-Care*	*Who Describes Arrangement?*	*Reliability of Description Assessed?*	*Variables*	*Negative Consequences for Self-Care Children Compared to Supervised Children?*
Felner (1992)			primarily Black		without adult supervision on a regular basis			classroom behavior, self-esteem, risk-taking	
Richardson, Radziszkewska, Dent, and Flay (1993)	Cross-sectional	Questionnaires	3,993 ninth graders; racially diverse	No	Unsupervised care after school	Child	No	Cigarette use, alcohol use, marijuana use, depressed mood, academic grades, risk-taking	Yes
Posner and Vandell (1994)	Cross-sectional	Questionnaires and interviews	216 third graders; urban, low income	No	Unsupervised after school for 3 days a week or more	Parents	Yes	Reading performance, academic achievement, conduct grades, peer relations, emotional	Yes

								adjustment, adult relations, work habits, behavior problems	
Cutler, Smith, and Kilmon (1995)	Cross-sectional	Questionnaires	154 fifth graders; 44% White, 33% Black, 23% Hispanic	No	Spend at least 2 hours each week at home alone without adult (>18 years old) supervision	Parent	No	Self-worth, scholastic competence, behavioral conduct, substance use, academic performance, school absenteeism	No
Mulhall, Stone, and Stone (1996)	Cross-sectional	Questionnaires	636 grade 5–7 students; 77% White, 15% Black; urban & rural areas	No	Child reported spending 2 or more days alone after school without adult supervision	Child	No	Substance use (alcohol, marijuana, inhalants, steroids, cigarettes, or smokeless tobacco), reported school grades	Yes

(continues)

TABLE 2.1 *(continued)*

Study	*Time Frame*	*Questionnaires/ Interviews*	*Sample*	*Excludes Nonemployed Parents?*	*Definition of Self-Care*	*Who Describes Arrangement?*	*Reliability of Description Assessed?*	*Variables*	*Negative Consequences for Self-Care Children Compared to Supervised Children?*
Pettit, Laird, Bates, and Dodge (1997)	Longitudinal	Questionnaires and interviews	466 fifth graders; racially and socioeconomically diverse, urban	No	Child comes home and takes care of him or herself or is taken care of by older sibling (nonadult)	Parent	No	Behavior problems, social competence with peers, academic performance	Yes
Marshall et al. (1997)	Cross-sectional	Questionnaires and interviews	206 Grade 1–4 students; racially and socioeconomically diverse, urban	No	Home alone or only with younger siblings and no adult, or with older siblings as caretakers (< 18 years old)	Parent	No	Behavioral adjustment	Yes, only for low-income children

Note: An earlier version of Table 2.1 appeared in Belle, D., Norell, S., and Lewis, A. (1997). Becoming unsupervised: Children's transitions from adult-care to self-care in the after-school hours. In I. Gotlib & B. Wheaton (Eds.) *Stress and adversity over the life course: Trajectories and turning points* (pp. 159–178). Cambridge: Cambridge University Press.

child's assignment to a particular after-school arrangement, rather than the other way around. This is one of the interpretations Woods offered when she found that heavy household responsibilities were associated with high intelligence and school achievement. Certainly, children are not randomly assigned to after-school arrangements, and several authors interpret at least some of their findings as illuminating the forces that contribute to the child's assignment. L. Steinberg (1986), for instance, found parental permissiveness associated with self-care after school (among boys) and with spending after-school time at a greater distance from home (among girls). Galambos and Maggs (1991b) found that parental acceptance was lower and conflict with parents was higher among self-care girls who spent after-school time away from home than among other girls. These patterns did not hold for boys, however. In fact, self-care boys who spent the after-school hours away from home actually had more accepting parents than other boys.

Stability of After-School Arrangements

Cross-sectional research that correlates after-school arrangements with child "outcomes" operates with the implicit assumption that after-school arrangements are sufficiently stable in children's lives that their "effects" can be assessed. Yet research has not addressed the stability of children's after-school arrangements. Parallel research on the stability over time of child-care arrangements for preschool children finds that instability is the norm: "most mothers change care arrangements frequently" (Floge, 1975, p. 143). Floge conducted a series of three interviews over a 4-year period with the mothers of preschool children. Of those mothers who were working or attending school at the first and second interview, only half used a similar child-care arrangement at both points in time. Of those mothers working or attending school at the second and third interview, only 8% were using the same type of child care at both times. Furthermore, changing child-care arrangements and using a combination of child-care arrangements rather than relying on a single type, were related to staying in the labor market or in school. Mothers who used only a single type of child care and those who did not change child-care arrangements were less likely to be working or attending school later in the study, suggesting that changing arrangements and using multiple arrangements was somehow conducive to or necessary for continued maternal employment.

Defining Supervision

Studies of children's after-school arrangements also define supervision in different ways, so that a child characterized as *supervised* in one study would appear as *unsupervised* in another. Lovko and Ullman (1989), for instance, considered a child unsupervised if he or she regularly spends as little as 30 minutes per week without supervision, whereas to be considered unsupervised in Posner and Vandell's (1994) research, a child would have to be in self-care for three or more afternoons a week, and in Messer, Wuensch, and Diamond's (1989) study, a child would have to be unsupervised 2 hours each day for 1 year. Potential providers of supervision are limited to adults in some studies, but may include children or adolescents of various ages in others. As Riley and Steinberg (1993) noted:

> A 10-year-old in the care of a 12-year-old sibling is considered "supervised" by both Steinberg (1986) and Cole and Rodman (1987), but "latchkey" by Cain and Hofferth (1989) and Vandell and Ramanan (1991). Vandell and Corasaniti's (1987) "latchkey" group could contain a third grader cared for by a 17-year-old. (p. 2)

Some studies define the unsupervised child as one who returns home to an empty house, whereas others include children who are unsupervised at other locations in the community.

Some researchers determine "supervision" from the presence of adult figures in the after-school setting whether or not these adults acknowledge any responsibility for the young people (L. Steinberg, 1986), whereas other researchers focus on the caretaking relationships that exist between adults and young people, whether or not the adults are physically present. Posner and Vandell (1994), for instance, asked parents whether their children's after-school arrangements should be characterized as maternal care, informal adult supervision, self-care, or formal after-school programs. When Posner and Vandell then investigated the presence of adults during the after-school hours for children categorized in these different arrangements they found that self-care children actually spent 73% of their after-school hours in the presence of adults, and that children in self-care did not differ from children in informal care in the amount of adult supervision they received.

Some researchers limit the self-care population to those children who are on their own because their parents are at work (Galambos & Maggs, 1991b; Rodman, Pratto, & Nelson, 1988), whereas other researchers base self-care status on the child's whereabouts after school, not the parents' (Richardson et al., 1989; L. Steinberg, 1986). In practice, this means that children can be considered unsupervised if they spend after-school time at the local shopping mall or park, even if their mothers or fathers are at home during that time. Rodman et al. (1988) questioned this practice, arguing that it confounds the issue of parental control style with the issue of parental absence as necessitated by employment. Although it is instructive to study the implications of parental control, such findings do not speak directly to the specific situation of children whose parents cannot be with them because they are at work.

L. Steinberg (1986), for instance, studied susceptibility to peer pressure among adolescents in Grades 5 through 9. Young people were categorized as adult-supervised, at home or elsewhere, or unsupervised, at home or elsewhere, on the basis of their "usual" situation after school. Although the children of nonemployed mothers were more likely than the children of employed mothers to spend after-school time at home with a parent or other adult, more than 60% of the children with nonemployed mothers were not found in this situation. This means that 60% of the children whose mothers were not employed potentially appeared in this study as unsupervised children.

Similarly, Richardson et al. (1989) examined alcohol, tobacco, and marijuana use among eighth-grade students who spent differing amounts of unsupervised time after school. Although the paper begins with an invocation of "recent changes in demographic and economic characteristics of American families" including the "increase in the number of families in which both parents work..." (p. 448), the employment status of parents is never assessed by these researchers. Self-care status is determined by questions such as, "How many days do you take care of yourself in the afternoon or evening after school without an adult being there?" Once again, it is possible that the children of nonemployed parents appear in this study as unsupervised young people.

Classification schemes for after-school arrangements often ask children or parents whether the children are supervised or unsupervised, leaving such perplexing definitional issues to the respondents and thus beyond the awareness of the researcher.

Reliability

Furthermore, most studies ask only one family member to describe the child's after-school arrangement and do not attempt to assess the reliability of this description. The reliability issue is not a trivial one, as is shown in the few studies that have assessed agreement between independent reports of the child's after-school arrangements. Woods (1972) found that maternal reports of the quality and quantity of substitute supervision and children's reports of the quantity of such supervision were significantly, but not highly, correlated (r = .35, p < .05). Only Berman, Winkleby, Chesterman, and Boyce (1992) had strongly encouraging results, finding perfect agreement in the sample of 11 families they telephoned to check the accuracy of the child's self-report of his or her primary (3 days per week or more) after-school arrangement.

Richardson et al. (1989), on the other hand, compared the reports of adolescents and their parents on the number of days per week, hours per day, and hours per week the adolescents spent in self-care. Although the adolescent and parent reports were significantly correlated, the Pearson r values only ranged between .31 and .42. And these values were obtained from the 44.3% of parents who returned questionnaires their children had brought home to them, not from the majority of parents who never returned the questionnaires. Interestingly, children were four times more likely than parents to report the higher number of hours spent in self-care, suggesting a substantial bias in reporting, depending on the informant chosen.

> It is possible that parents minimize the number of hours they leave their children either because they underestimate the actual number of hours or they want to enhance their own self-image as a parent. On the other hand, children may systematically overestimate the number of hours they are alone because the time appears to be longer than it actually is or they wish to appear more mature. (Richardson et al., 1989, p. 564)

Weisner and Gallimore (1977) described an observational study of Hawaiian-American children after school in their homes and neighborhoods that actually compares children's self-reports of their supervision status to those of trained observers. After each observation period, the child was asked, "Is anyone taking care of you?" Substantial disagreement was found between the children's responses and the judgments of the observers. Weisner and Gallimore (1977) offered possible explanations for these discrepancies, but refused to label one set of reporters accurate and the other biased.

> Girls seem to underreport times when they are not being cared for, while boys overreport. Or are our criteria for inferring caretaking structure wrong, so that it is the observers who are (differentially) over- and underreporting? (p. 187)

The authors speculated that girls may be more sensitive to caretaking relationships and that boys may prefer to think of themselves and present themselves to others as autonomous and independent.

Terminology

Even terminology is controversial. Galambos and Maggs (1991a) objected to the phrase *latchkey child* both because it implies that unsupervised children stay in their homes, although many do not, and because it suggests that unsupervised children are lonely and neglected. Several writers, including Galambos and Maggs, prefer the phrase *self-care child*, which others reject as an oxymoron. Perhaps the least emotionally loaded term is *unsupervised children*.

Quality

In most published research, supervision is simply a dichotomous variable, with no attention paid to the characteristics of supervision that might make it more or less supportive to children. Recently, however, Rosenthal and Vandell (1996) assessed the quality of after-school programs, and Marshall et al. (1997) sampled the range of activities engaged in by children in a variety of after-school settings, not including self- or sibling-care. Such variations do make a difference to children.

Process

Finally, very few studies go beyond correlating aspects of children's after-school arrangements with indices of child well-being to explore the processes by which after-school arrangements might affect children's well-being. Without some understanding of the mechanisms that are involved, it is difficult to make sense of unexpected findings or to develop a comprehensive understanding of the impact of after-school arrangements on children.

RESEARCH FINDINGS

Given the methodological diversity and limitations of the studies, it is not surprising that they have produced no clear consensus about the significance of after-school supervision for children whose parents are at work. Some studies report problems for unsupervised children, others find no differences between supervised and unsupervised children, and credible studies have reported poorer outcomes for children who spend after-school time with older siblings, babysitters, after-school teachers, and their own mothers, than for children who spend after-school time on their own.

Several of the negative outcomes have been found for adolescent, rather than younger children and in studies that include young people with nonemployed parents. Richardson et al. (1989), for instance, found that eighth graders who spent more than 11 hours per week in self-care were at twice the risk of using alcohol, tobacco, and marijuana as young people who were never unsupervised. Interestingly, the self-care adolescents were more likely than the supervised adolescents to have parents who themselves used alcohol and tobacco. L. Steinberg (1986) found that unsupervised fifth through ninth graders who spent after-school time at home were no more susceptible to peer pressure than those who were supervised by parents at home. However, adolescents who spent unsupervised after-school time at a friend's house or "hanging out" were more susceptible to peer pressure than either of the at-home groups.

Several studies of younger children have not found deficits among unsupervised children. In a particularly comprehensive investigation, Vandell and Corasaniti (1988) compared third-grade self-care children with children who spent after-school time at home with their mothers, at home with sitters, or in formal after-school programs. Reports from parents, teachers, children's peers and the children themselves revealed no differences between self-care and mother-care children in the large array of variables studied. However, children who attended after-school programs were viewed more negatively by peers, made lower academic grades and had lower standardized test scores than mother-care or self-care children, and children who stayed with sitters after school were viewed less favorably by their peers than the self-care or mother-care children. The authors speculated that the findings may reflect the poor quality of many of the after-school programs, stigma attending their use, or a self-selection factor, in which only those children viewed by parents as needing adult supervision are assigned to center care. In this cross-sectional study, as in others, the presumed outcomes of after-school arrangements may, in fact, have led to differential assignment to after-school arrangements.

In another study with an unexpected outcome, Berman et al. (1992) found no deficits in self-competence scores among fourth and sixth graders who cared for themselves after school. The authors did find, however, that children cared for after school by older siblings reported significantly lower self-competence scores in the domains of global self-worth, social acceptance, and physical appearance compared to children cared for after school by adults and children in self-care.

Perhaps the most counterintuitive finding was reported by Vandell and Ramanan (1991), who studied supervision arrangements among third, fourth, and fifth graders from the National Longitudinal Study of Youth. Most of these children were born to teenage mothers, and almost half lived in households with incomes below the poverty line, making this an economically stressed research sample. The authors found the lowest levels of adjustment and well-being among children cared for by their own mothers after school. This group also experienced more poverty and less emotional support than did other groups of children in the study. Latchkey arrangements were associated with some negative effects, but these disappeared when controls were introduced for family income and for emotional support.

It is also possible that negative effects of unsupervised time in the early school years become clearer and easier to detect as time goes by. In a thoughtful longitudinal study that controls for the child's adjustment level in kindergarten and assesses the impact of unsupervised time during Grades 1, 3, and 5 on outcomes in Grade 6, Pettit, Laird, Bates, and Dodge (1997) showed striking negative effects of early unsupervised time on social competence, achievement test scores, grade point averages, and externalizing behavior problems, with stronger effects for unsupervised time in Grades 1 and 3 than in Grade 5.

Location and Monitoring

Research also suggests that the nature of after-school supervision may not be the most crucial variable to consider. Instead, the location at which children spend unsupervised time and "distal" supervision by parents who monitor the child's after-school activities may be more critical aspects of the child's after-school experience. As mentioned previously, Steinberg (1986) found that self-care children who "hung out" at settings away from home reported themselves more susceptible to peer pressure to engage in antisocial behavior than either adult-supervised children or self-care children who spent after-school time at their own homes. Similarly, children whose parents did not know their whereabouts after school were more susceptible to negative peer pressure than those who were more closely monitored.

Galambos and Maggs (1991b) replicated and extended Steinberg's work by showing that sixth-grade children in self-care at home were as unlikely to get into trouble as children supervised by adults after school. Boys showed no effects of self-care in any situation. However, girls without adult supervision who spent after-school hours away from their homes engaged in more problem behaviors than did at-home or adult-supervised girls. Furthermore, Galambos and Maggs demonstrated this result in a sample carefully limited to the children of dual-earner families and in one of the only longitudinal studies of after-school arrangements yet published. The authors reported the effects of self-care at one point in time on child behavior 6 months later.

When Howard, Broquet, and Farrell (1991) examined the impact of after-school arrangements on more than 1,000 predominantly Black and low-income seventh-grade students, they found that whether or not students spent after school hours with an adult failed to predict any of their behavioral outcomes. But students who spent after-school hours away from home, whether or not supervised by an adult, reported lower school grades and poorer school attendance records and were more likely to engage in drug use, minor and major delinquency, and sexual intercourse than children at home after school. Both boys and girls demonstrated such effects. Adult supervision was important, however, in predicting emotional and personality variables. When away from adults after school, students reported more distress and depression and lower levels of self-esteem and self-reliance.

Type of Community and Family Socioeconomic Status

Research also suggests that the risks associated with unsupervised time may differ between rural/suburban and urban areas and between poor and middle-class communities. Several studies that found no deficits associated with unsupervised time were conducted in middle-class rural or suburban areas (Galambos & Garbarino, 1985; Lovko & Ullman, 1989; Vandell & Corasaniti, 1988), whereas studies demonstrating problems associated with unsupervised time were often carried out in low-income urban areas (Long & Long, 1982; Posner & Vandell, 1994; Woods, 1972).

In a recent analysis, Marshall et al. (1997) discovered that the risks of unsupervised time were limited to those children in their study whose families earned less than the median income for the sample. Such children showed higher levels of externalizing behavior problems when they spent unsupervised time after school and lower levels of internalizing problems when they attended after-school programs. In contrast, there was no relation between type of after-school care and behavioral adjustment for children whose families had incomes above the median for the sample.

Similarly, Pettit et al. (1997) found that self-care after school was associated with externalizing problems only among children from low socioeconomic status (SES) families. For children from higher SES families, the extent of externalizing problems did not vary with the amount of time spent in self-care. However, self-care was associated with poorer academic outcomes and lower social competence irrespective of SES. Pettit and his colleagues also reported that although higher SES children showed no variation in later adjustment based on their involvement in day care after school, children from low SES families had higher levels of social competence and lower levels of both internalizing and externalizing problems in sixth grade when they spent more time in day-care programs after school during their first-grade year.

The striking convergence of these two methodologically rigorous studies lends further credence to the proposition that unsupervised after-school time poses particular dangers to children from low-income families.

Social Support Issues

In attempting to explain the wide variation in responses to unsupervised after-school time, several researchers have examined ways in which social support resources might moderate the impact of particular after-school arrangements. In fact, several of the previously discussed research findings can be interpreted within a social support framework. Steinberg's finding that "distal supervision" by parents was associated with positive outcomes for children might be interpreted in this light, such supervision at a distance conveying to the child the sense of parental concern.

Berman et al.'s (1992) finding that poor self-esteem is associated with sibling care and not self-care certainly flies in the face of the simplistic notion that what children need after school is simply more companionship. In attempting to make sense of this finding, Berman cited the research literature on siblings as caretakers, noting that their interactions with younger children tend to be harsher and less attuned to the developmental needs of the children than are the interactions of adults. Such sibling care may actually supply little support to younger children.

Similarly, Vandell and Ramanan's finding that mother-care children fare poorly is surprising if one expects that mother presence will equal support from mother. As these authors showed, emotional support to children cannot always be inferred from the simple presence of a potential support provider. When emotional support is directly assessed, its importance for children's well-being becomes apparent.

Brown, Pratto, and Rodman (1989) theorized that communication during after-school hours between parents and their self-care children would have a positive impact on the mother's satisfaction with the child's self-care arrangements. They found, however, contrary to their hypotheses, that mothers who had daily telephone contact with their self-care children and mothers who left instructions for their self-care children were actually less satisfied with their children's after-school arrangements than mothers who lacked such forms of parent–child communication. Once again self-selection may be the explanation, as parents may well communicate more often with self-care children perceived to need this attention more urgently. Yet the findings of this study suggest that the simple existence of communication between parent and child may not actually convey support.

Gender

Gender may play an important role in determining the significance of self-care, with most studies suggesting that girls are at greater risk than boys in a self-care situation. Interestingly, this reverses the pattern of research findings on gender differences in response to maternal employment. In that research tradition, studies more often find boys to be at higher risk than girls when mothers are employed (Crouter, MacDermid, McHale, & Perry-Jenkins, 1990). Woods (1972) reported marked deficits in cognitive functioning and social relations among girls, but not boys, who were unsupervised during summer vacation and during three key periods of the school day (breakfast, lunch, and after school). L. Steinberg (1986) discovered that girls who lacked adult supervision after school scored higher than supervised girls on a measure of susceptibility to peer pressure, whereas lack of supervision had no such direct effect on boys. Galambos and Maggs (1991b) found that girls who had spent unsupervised time away from home associated more with deviant peers and reported a higher number of problem behaviors than girls who were unsupervised at home or those who had supervision after school. There was no comparable effect of self-care for boys.

However, in their sample of fifth and sixth graders from a rural college town, Diamond, Kataria, and Messer (1989) noted that self-care was only associated with negative outcomes for boys. Boys who were unsupervised every day after school were described by their parents and described themselves as having more behavioral problems than boys who spent less unsupervised time or boys who spent after-school time with older siblings or adults. In contrast, girls who spent each afternoon unsupervised were rated by parents as having fewer behavioral problems than adult-supervised girls, perhaps because parents only permitted daughters they viewed as especially well adjusted to spend unsupervised time after school.

CONCLUSION

Most discussions of children's lives after school begin with the assumption that lack of supervision is problematic for children. Yet the empirical research has produced unexpected findings. Some studies report problems for unsupervised children, others find no differences between supervised and unsupervised children, and credible studies have reported poorer outcomes for children who spend after-school time with older siblings, babysitters, after-school teachers. and their own mothers, than for children who spend after-school time on their own.

There are suggestions in the literature that lack of supervision is more harmful to some children than to others. Girls, urban children, and children in low-income communities more often seem to experience problems associated with lack of supervision than do boys, suburban children, and children in economically secure communities. There is also the suggestion that the risks of unsupervised time do not diminish with age. If anything, more clear-cut dangers have been documented for adolescent children than for those in the early elementary school years.

Yet such findings are suspect because no study randomly assigns children to after-school arrangements and very few follow children over time. Causal ordering is therefore unclear. It is possible that some of the reported outcomes of lack of supervision actually reflect the factors that precipitate lack of supervision in the first place. Several studies suggest that parents who allow their children to be unsupervised in the after-school hours differ from those who insist on supervision, or that the parent–child relationship differs between supervised children and those who are unsupervised. Could some of the research findings reflect differences in families or in parent–child relationships that lead both to differences in supervision status and to differences in the reported outcomes of supervision? If so, supervision status would be epiphenomenal, having no causal importance itself in producing successful or unsuccessful outcomes for young people. Problems in defining supervision, and inconsistencies among reporters in describing supervision, also suggest that considerable caution is warranted.

The research comparing latchkey to supervised children has thus suggested some fascinating complexities. It has not yet provided a definitive account of the significance to children of supervision, or absence of supervision, in the after-school hours.

3

A Different Approach to the Question

The study described here pries open the black box of supervised and unsupervised after-school care to provide a richer understanding of the ways children actually spend their time after school before working parents return home. The research asks how after-school arrangements come about and how children respond to their diverse after-school experiences. A 4-year longitudinal study with annual interviews was undertaken to assess the changes over time that are hidden when cross-sectional research takes "snapshots" of children at a single point in time. Both children and parents were interviewed to compare and contrast their perspectives.

RESEARCH FAMILIES

Participation in the study was limited to families with parents employed or in school full time and with at least one child in elementary school at the start of the study. (In two-parent families both parents had to be working full time, and in single-parent families the solo parent had to be working full time.) Families were selected to be diverse in SES, ethnicity, and family structure, and were recruited through schools, after-school programs, housing projects, and community organizations. Low-income and single-parent families were intentionally overrepresented as it was anticipated that such families would have unique difficulties in creating satisfactory after-school arrangements for the children. Families were paid $50 for each round of interviews.

Recruitment was difficult. Almost by definition, parents who work full time are busy, and I was grateful to those willing to devote a weekend afternoon or midweek evening to interview questions. The requirement that both parents and children participate in the study and that they all remain involved for several years may have discouraged others. In addition, some parents or children may have been uncomfortable discussing their after-school arrangements or may have been skeptical of our assurances of confidentiality.

In the first year of field work, 39 families were successfully recruited and interviewed. The second year, an additional 14 families were recruited, for a total of 53. Families were then reinterviewed annually. The original 39 families were interviewed for 4 years, whereas the families added in the second year of the study completed three rounds of interviewing before the study's completion. Attrition from the study was minimal, with all but one family finishing the study. An additional three families each missed one round of interviewing, but returned to the study the following year. In several cases, families moved out of the area during the period of the study and all were successfully reinterviewed, either in their new homes, on their visits to the Boston area, or over the telephone (in the case of one family that had moved overseas).

Of the 53 families in the study, 16 were African American, 1 was Hispanic, 1 was Asian American, and 35 were non-Hispanic White. (For the families in the study that included people of different races, we based the racial categorization on the race of the mother. In one of the families we categorized as African American, for instance, the father was non-Hispanic White. In one of the families we categorized as White, the mother's resident boyfriend was African American. In yet another non-Hispanic White family, the focus child was adopted, and was African American.) One third of the families had annual incomes below $20,000 at the start of the study, one third had incomes in the $20,000 to $30,000 range, and one third had incomes of more than $30,000. All but 2 mothers had high school degrees or GEDs, more than half had completed a college education, and 15 held advanced degrees.

In each family, we focused on one child who was attending elementary school, typically the youngest elementary school child in the household. These children (30 girls, 23 boys) ranged in age at the start of the study from 7 to 12. At the start of the study, 21 children lived with two parents, 27 with a single parent, and 5 children lived in joint-custody families in which the child divided time between the mother's and the father's household. In all but one single-parent family, the solo parent was the mother. Over the course of the study, one parent died, four couples divorced or separated, two single parents married or began living with a romantic partner, and five babies were born. These family changes were, of course, highly significant in their own right, and they also often led to changes in children's after-school arrangements.

All families resided initially in the greater Boston area, most in two communities in which the heaviest recruitment took place. These two communities in some ways represented a "best case" scenario for children's after-school arrangements. At the time of the study, they were among the the small minority (22%) of Massachusetts communities that provided before- or after-school programs through the schools (Commonwealth of Massachusetts Special Legislative Commission on Children in Need of Services, 1989). In addition, most after-school programs in these communities had been operating for several years before the start of this study, and many subsidized the cost of care for children from low-income families. In contrast, a national study funded by the U.S. Department of Education found that the average before- and after-school program sponsored by a public school was just over 6 years old in 1993 and that most programs failed to offer sliding fee scales, scholarships, or tuition grants (National Study of Before and After School Programs, 1993).

Families lived in communities the census would describe as urban, although some neighborhoods had a spacious, suburban feel. Compared to most communities throughout the country, the communities studied here were generally well served by public transportation, although some families were located much more conveniently than others. Not all children in the study attended their neighborhood schools. One of the communities in which we worked allowed parents to choose any of the community's schools for their children and provided school bus transportation to and from school. Other children attended private schools or participated in arrangements that transported city children to suburban schools.

RESEARCH PROCEDURES

Interviewers visited families in teams, with a separate interviewer assigned to each person to be interviewed. Efforts were made to pair the same interviewers and interviewees over all the years of the study, although this often was not possible. About half of all research participants had the same interviewer for at least two rounds of interviewing. I conducted a substantial number of interviews myself (66 interviews concentrated in 32 of the research families), and virtually all the remaining interviewers were doctoral students in psychology or education. Before conducting any interviews with research families, all interviewers received training and successfully completed practice interviews with families not included in the study. Research group meetings were held on a frequent basis, often weekly, to plan interview visits, correct problems, and discuss insights that arose.

The first visit to each research family was arranged so that parents and children could meet together with their interviewers, discuss the nature of the study, and provide informed consent. Informed consent statements were discussed with both parents and children present so that parents could be certain that their children understood and agreed to the procedures of the study. In addition to allowing family members an opportunity to read the informed consent material, interviewers verbally emphasized to children the key points of the statement, especially the child's right to end the interview at any point and to decline to answer any interview question for any reason. Families were asked to choose a code name by which their family would be known to the research group. The ensuing discussion was often fun, and helped to concretize for children our promise of privacy and confidentiality. No family was interviewed until parents had given their informed consent for their own participation and for that of their children, and children had given their informed assent to participate.

Family members were then interviewed separately about the child's after-school routine, social support network, emotional well-being, and behavioral adjustment. Information was also gathered on the daily schedules and whereabouts of all household members. In each family, the focus child and one parent, usually the mother, were interviewed each year. Annual interviews were also conducted with interested fathers and often with those siblings who spent after-school time with a focus child. Interviews included both open-ended questions and standardized questionnaires, lasted between 1 and 2 hours, and were generally conducted in the family's home. On occasion, interviews were conducted at my Boston University research offices, a parent's work place, or another setting chosen by the research family. Interviewers did their best to assure that interviews were conducted privately, although in some cases the arrangements of small apartments made complete privacy impossible. In many cases as well, younger children had to be attended to during the course of interviews. Watching the ways in which parents and children handled the demands of these children while attempting to complete their interviews gave us additional insight into the experience of family life.

THE RESEARCH INTERVIEWS

Open-ended questions were used to elicit rich and detailed information about the child's after-school arrangements. Children were asked questions such as:

- "Could you start by telling me how you usually spend your time after school lets out and before your parent(s) come(s) home?"
- "Is every day the same or is it different on different days of the week? On which days do you do which things (after-school program, lessons, home alone, sports, etc.)?" (Cite hours to best of child's ability.)
- "Who are you with in each situation or are you by yourself?"

These questions were followed by a series of additional questions asking children about their likes and dislikes in the after-school hours, social supports available in the after-school hours, rules governing after-school time, and so on. Parents were asked similar questions about the child's after-school arrangement, such as," Does (s/he) do the same thing after school each day, or does her/his arrangement differ by the day of the week?" Parents were also asked how their children's after-school arrangements came about, and about liked and disliked aspects of the child's after-school arrangements, communication with the child during the after-school period, rules for the after-school hours, and so on. Interviewers were instructed to probe for complete responses to each interview question and to pursue additional points that parents and children raised.

Certain topics were raised in only 1 or 2 years of the study. Only in Year 1, for instance, were parents asked to describe all of the child's after-school arrangements since beginning kindergarten or to reflect on their own childhood after-school arrangements. In Year 4 of the study we asked parents and children about their initial reasons for participation in the study, what they had liked and disliked about the research, and whether being in the study had affected their own thinking and actions regarding after-school arrangements.

Each year of the study, mothers responded to standardized measures assessing the child's behavioral adjustment (Achenbach & Edelbrock, 1983) and experience of life events (Coddington, 1984). In addition, mothers rated on a 10-point scale how much "worry, upset, or concern" they themselves experienced in 13 realms of life: finances, parenting, child's after-school arrangements, marriage or love relationship, housing, neighborhood, work (if currently employed), lack of work (if currently unemployed), friends, relatives, physical health, mental health, and education. They also responded to the Network Orientation scale (Vaux, Burda, & Stewart, 1986), which assesses the extent to which an individual believes that turning to others in times of difficulty is useful, advisable, and safe. Fathers completed interviews that were identical to those given to mothers, except that fathers were not asked to complete the Child Behavior Checklist.

The Children's Inventory of Social Support (Wolchik, Beals, & Sandler, 1989) was used each year to investigate the child's receipt of social support resources from different people and the child's satisfaction with that support. Children were asked to list all of the individuals who provided support to them in the realms of recreation, advice and information, goods and services, emotional support, and positive feedback, as well as those individuals with whom they had negative interactions, and to rate their level of satisfaction with support from family members and from those outside the family. Children also responded each year to a set of brief, standardized measures assessing loneliness (Asher, Hymel, & Renshaw, 1984), self-esteem (Coopersmith, 1967), locus of control (Nowicki & Strickland, 1973), and network orientation (Vaux et al., 1986).

After conducting each interview, the interviewer wrote field notes describing the interview, the circumstances in which it was conducted (such as any lapse in privacy), and any significant conversations that occurred before or after the formal interview. Interviewers also highlighted salient points in the interview concerning the child's after-school experiences and social supports.

EVOLUTION OF THE PROJECT

Like many research projects, particularly those that take place over several years, this research project changed over time. Early research difficulties led to changes in study design, and the difficulties were sometimes later conceptualized as research findings!

We had originally planned to interview only the mother and a single child in each research family. When a sympathetic and involved father in one of the research families challenged this sexist exclusion of the male parent, we reconceptualized our mission and sought out the perspectives of fathers as well as mothers. We sought out the views of siblings to the focus children when we were convinced that these additional perspectives would also be valuable.

Initially, our study was designed to contrast three distinct groups of children who had been described in previous research: those supervised after school by adults, those supervised after school by nonadult siblings, and those children who were unsupervised after school. Recruitment efforts quickly revealed, however, that the world of after-school arrangements was more complex than we had anticipated. When a family registered interest in the study and was found to be eligible we then asked what the child did after school. To our surprise, parents rarely described a single arrangement as typical of the entire school week. Instead, they would often tell us something like, "Well, on Monday she has soccer practice, on Tuesday she is home by herself, on Wednesday and Thursday she goes to a friend's house, and on Friday I come home early from work to be with her." Initially, we tried to preserve our categorical system, looking for families in which a child was either in adult care, sibling care, or self-care at least 3 days a week. This hope died, too, as families continued to describe arrangements that varied significantly from day to day. We eventually decided to abandon the category system, to take all families as they came, and to examine the reasons for so much complexity.

In most investigations, children's after-school arrangements are categorized based on what children "usually" do. This practice fails to capture the variety of many children's after-school experiences, a variety often specifically planned for by parents and the children themselves.

We had further problems when parents and children described to us after-school arrangements that seemed to challenge the neat distinction we thought we had understood between supervision and self-care. We puzzled over how to categorize the arrangements of 7-year-old Meiguei Chen, for instance, who spends her after-school time in the children's room of her town's public library. Although adult librarians are present and, in fact, unofficially keep an eye on Meiguei, they have no formal responsibility for her.

Another situation that challenged our category system is that of Cynthia Edwards, whose mother is always at home when 8-year-old Cynthia returns from school each day. But Cynthia's mother is almost always asleep, because she works the night shift as a nurse. Cynthia knows she can awaken her mother in an emergency, but that otherwise she should let her mother get the rest she needs before her nighttime job.

Thinking about such children's experiences made us confront a marginal area between supervised and self-care arrangements. Either/or categorization here ignores complexities that figure largely in child and adult perceptions of these after-school arrangements.

RECOGNIZING ALTERNATE PERSPECTIVES

Most research on children's after-school arrangements has determined those arrangements from the statements of a single family member, either the child or a parent. In our study, in contrast, we asked each family member we interviewed to describe and discuss what the child did after school. Because we generally interviewed all of the family members on the same occasion, research group members often compared notes and discussed their interviews soon after they were conducted. Although we had intentionally sought out the viewpoints of multiple family members, we were unprepared for the pervasive discrepancies we found. In the Jackson family, for instance, Shirley Jackson, whom I interviewed in the first year of the study, told me that her 9-year-old daughter Martha attends an after-school program that she has attended for the previous 2 years, and that she will not be eligible to attend the following year. Shirley is generally satisfied with the program because it is a safe environment for Martha. "I feel it's a happy arrangement." The program provides painting and art projects ("making of objects from egg crates and that kind of thing"), a weekly visit to the aged, trips to museums and farms, music, and drama.

Shirley is concerned, however, that the program does not provide enough physical activities for the children. The broad age span of the children the program serves makes it difficult to do projects that interest all the children. As a result, not all of the activities are interesting for Martha, who is on the older side of the age spectrum. Shirley also complains of the high teacher turnover rate, which she relates to the low salary levels. On the other hand, after-school care is expensive. "If you had more than one child it would really be costly." Yet, she believes that "you get what you pay for." She wonders if the program is fulfilling the children's needs and comments that perhaps programs should allow kids more time out in the afternoons, rather than scheduling so many activities. When asked if Martha is satisfied with the program, Shirley says that Martha "groans and complains, but when I get there she seems happy." Shirley also says that Martha is a "TV freak" who would rather be watching television than attending the after-school program. I was impressed with the thoughtfulness of Shirley's responses, and the complexities that parents consider, even when their children are doing something as straightforward as attending a formal after-school program 5 days a week.

While I had this conversation with Shirley Jackson, my colleague interviewed her daughter in an adjacent room of their apartment just a few feet away. At the start of the interview, Martha stated that she attended her after-school program 2 days a week, attended a class 1 day a week, and came home to the Jackson apartment after school on the other days. Martha talked about spending time after school visiting her mother at work, hanging out with friends in the school yard, and going to friends' houses after school. On the afternoon before the interview, for instance, Martha described coming right home after school and spending 1 hour on the steps of the house with her grandmother (who lives with them) and her nephew. Afterward, she watched television by herself (although her grandmother was in the house) until her mother returned from work.

Martha was adamant that she liked nothing about her after-school program. "It stinks." She said that she has had "8 or 11" after-school teachers in 1 year, and has to do the same activities again and again.

> You have to go outside when you don't want to, and most of the choices are made by the little kids in the program. You have to go to the home for the aged even if you don't want to, and do things you've already done in art classes. The teachers are mean and unfair, use physical punishments, like grabbing a child by the neck, and if you bring a toy to after-school, you have to share it with the whole after-school. They say they will do something different next month, but it never happens. If one child is bad and is punished, the children are all punished.

Martha says she likes the time she spends at home and the time she spends at her mother's work very much, but strongly dislikes her after-school program. Later in the same interview, Martha says that she no longer attends the after-school program and that she has not gone in "a long time." According to Martha, just the week before the interview, her mother decided she did not have to go to the after-school program any more.

When my colleague and I compared notes after this set of interviews we struggled to understand how Martha and her mother could have such different perceptions or could offer us such different interpretations of reality. Each was aware that the other was being asked similar questions about Martha's after-school arrangements, and the interviews were actually going on simultaneously! We wondered if Martha had entirely stopped attending the program, and if so, whether Shirley knew or approved of this. Perhaps Shirley gave Martha permission to skip the program temporarily, and Martha interpreted this as permission to leave permanently. At any rate, each respondent appeared content with her own interpretation of the situation.

In the second year of the study, Marguerite Berger stopped attending her after-school program and began to stay home with her grandmother instead. According to Marguerite, this change came about because her mother changed jobs, leaving her position at the housing complex where the after-school program was located. According to Carol Berger, however, the change came about as a result of Marguerite's problematic behavior in school. She had failed a grade and was having problems dealing with the other children. Marguerite says she loves being with her grandmother and says her favorite time of day is after school (because she does not have to see her teacher any more), but Carol thinks Marguerite dislikes the present arrangement very much. On other aspects of family life there is extraordinary agreement. In Year 3, when asked how her mother shows her love, Marguerite says, "She yells at me when I do something wrong." When asked how she shows love to Marguerite, Carol says, "I hate to say this, but I yell at her." Marguerite also says she watches a lot of television (from 3 to 11 p.m. after school each day) and declares herself a "couch potato." According to Carol, Marguerite is a "television junkie."

Although we were initially dismayed to uncover discrepancies in the ways family members described the child's after-school arrangements, we came to appreciate that such discrepancies were not simply "noise" disguising a single, clear reality. We came to believe that differences in the ways family members perceived and described topics like after-school arrangements revealed crucial dynamics of family life and offered us new ways of appreciating the complexity of family experiences.

Sometimes the different wishes and values about after-school time are reconciled in families when parents and children adopt different understandings of the child's actual after-school time use or the reasons for it. This "reality stretch" may reduce tension between parents and children, each of whom is satisfied with a "reality" somewhat discrepant from that perceived by the other. We noticed these discrepancies particularly when children seemed to be withdrawing from after-school programs and beginning to spend more time on their own. Parents may have felt it was socially unacceptable to allow their children unsupervised time and they may have minimized the extent of such time to an interviewer who might be disapproving. However, if they truly meant to mislead us, they must have realized that this enterprise was futile, because we were also interviewing their children, often at the very same time that we were interviewing them. Rather than wishing intentionally to mislead us, we often felt that parents offered us the reality they attempted to believe in themselves.

In addition to parent–child disagreements, we also encountered husbands and wives who presented to us conflicting visions of their child's after-school arrangements. Although some discrepancies suggested that one parent was simply more involved or knowledgeable about the child's day, others seemed less innocuous. In two families, the father described a child as fully supervised during the after-school hours, while the mother described the child as spending substantial unsupervised time each week and described herself as highly distressed by the child's vulnerability when on his own. These two couples were two of the four who separated or divorced during the course of the study. Although the small numbers involved should restrain speculation, it seems plausible that serious discrepancies in the reports of fathers and mothers can reflect a troubling lack of shared vision about family life.

Variation in the way a family is experienced by its individual members has become a major theme in much contemporary, "postmodern" family research. As Stacey (1991) noted,

> Any unitary family history imposes arbitrary order upon the multiple, and often contradictory, subjectivities of the individuals whose diverse narratives it attempts to distill. It masks, thereby, those telling discrepancies between the His and Her marriages, as well as the Yours and Mine parent, child, sibling, and extended kin relationships that all families contain. (p. 183)

Such discrepancies emerged when Larson and Richards (1994) equipped mothers, fathers, and adolescents with electronic pagers that would signal them simultaneously several times a day over the course of a week. Family members were then to respond to standardized questionnaires concerning their activities, thoughts, and emotions just before the beep. Family members showed a low rate of agreement even in describing whether they were "with" another family member when they were beeped. On half the occasions that a mother or teenager described herself as with the other, the second person did not agree. Nor were spouses always in accord on this most basic observation. Such findings led Larson and Richards to argue that within families "interpretation of the most basic events may be contested" (p. viii) and to title their book about the emotional experiences of individuals in families, *Divergent Realities*.

IMPACT ON FAMILIES

When we returned to the Edwards family for our second round of interviews, Terry Edwards told us that talking with the interviewer the previous year had made her feel that her daughter, Cynthia, needed at least one supervised, structured activity during the week, and she had approached her ex-husband for the money to enroll their daughter in one weekly activity. Terry's comment made us realize that, just as our ideas were changed by our contacts with the research families, the parents and children we interviewed might be affected too.

At the end of the study, when we asked parents and children about such effects, we found that more than one third of the children and well over half of the mothers believed that being in the study had affected their thinking about children's after-school arrangements. One fourth of the mothers and a handful of children said that being in the study had led their family to do something differently, often simply to talk more about after-school arrangements. One child said being in the study had made him realize how lucky he is to have a lot of friends and things to do. Another said it made him think of more exciting things he could do after school. One child said that being in the study had made him realize that he should talk more to people about his problems.

Several mothers said that the interviews had made them more aware of their children's experiences and perceptions. As one mother said, "It focused my attention on what it is like for my kids after school." Another mother noted that she used to feel that the problem of after-school care was hers alone. "I think the study made me realize that we weren't struggling alone with this issue and stimulated thoughts of alternative solutions."

In some cases, mothers whose children spent unsupervised time were reassured by their participation in the study. One mother said, "I think more positively about it and do not consider the absence of supervision as a handicap or anything I have to apologize for. [The study] has given more dignity to our circumstances." Other mothers felt that the interview experience made them more aware of problems in the after-school hours, including problems they could do nothing about. One mother said that being in the study had made her think more about safety issues. Yet another pointed out, "I can't change my cash situation."

STRENGTHS AND WEAKNESSES OF THE RESEARCH METHOD

The research method chosen for this study—intensive, qualitative, and longitudinal interview research involving multiple respondents within each research family, and a relatively small and heterogeneous set of families—has particular weaknesses and strengths. Studies with larger and more representative samples are more appropriate for estimating the frequency of events, behaviors, and opinions in the general population. The current study is best equipped to illuminate complexities that are hidden in larger scale, less intensive research, to investigate processes that unfold over time or within families, and to capture the ways in which individuals make meaning of their experiences. Qualitative research can often generate new hypotheses, which can then be tested in quantitative studies later on, and, as is seen in later chapters, this study does suggest several directions for future research on children's after-school arrangements.

READING ABOUT PARTICULAR CHILDREN AND FAMILIES

In this text, the names of children and parents are pseudonyms, used to protect the privacy of the research participants. Occasionally an inessential detail about a child or a family that might reveal the child's real-life identity is changed. Otherwise, information given in this text is accurate in describing the 53 research families in the study. The appendix at the end of the text gives demographic information about each of the 53 children in the study.

4

Dilemmas

> *Time use by children is often the product of so many constraints that we must carefully consider our own biases and perspectives before making judgments. In describing differences in time-use behavior, we are trying to gain some appreciation for the complexity and difficulty of day-to-day life, which may make choices that run counter to conventional wisdom seem very rational indeed.*
>
> —Medrich et al. (1982, p. 8)

Employed parents must scramble these days to provide acceptable after-school arrangements for their children. A flexible job, a sympathetic employer, a supportive relative, or a terrific after-school program may smooth the way, but for most employed parents providing satisfactory after-school arrangements for children remains a challenge. Responses to this challenge differ, reflecting parents' differing resources, values, and experiences. Many families settle for arrangements they do not like, because they can find no real alternatives. Even arrangements that work well for a time, often prove disappointing later on. Children change, programs change, and re-adjustments are required.

Stephanie Samuels wonders if people realize what an "emotional issue" it is for parents to make after-school arrangements for their children.

> You're in a situation where you don't have a choice. You have to provide some kind of [care] for your child, and no arrangement will ever be perfect.

> I think there's always an element of guilt about putting a child in a program. "Should I be there? What is the child missing?"

As Terry Edwards experiences it, "All I do after 3:00 is worry."

Yet, after-school arrangements are necessary because parents must work. Carol Berger sees her daughter's after-school program as essential. "It's either that or staying home on welfare." At the other end of the income spectrum, the Martells initially thought about sending their child to one of the private schools that had accepted her for kindergarten, but none of these schools offered full after-school programs. They decided instead to send their daughter to the public school, which did have such a program.

LOOKING BACKWARD

The dilemmas parents face today may feel particularly difficult because they often represent a striking departure from the way family life was experienced a generation ago, when fewer mothers worked outside the home, more households included two parents, and children often had more siblings. As Hawkins and Crouter (1991) noted, "Many of the parents of contemporary young adults married and raised children in a historically unique period of time when economic and social conditions exempted most married women from contributing economically to the family" (p. 211). Few parents today can simply assume that their children's after-school time will be spent the way they spent their own afternoons.

We asked each of the parents we interviewed whether their own mothers were employed full time when they were the same age as their children are now, whether arrangements for their children are similar to or different from what they experienced themselves growing up, and whether when they made after-school arrangements for their children they thought about their own experiences growing up and tried to make arrangements that were like or unlike what they experienced.

Only one third of the parents we interviewed reported that their own mothers were employed full time when they were children, although among African-American respondents the figure was higher: Half had mothers who were employed full time. Eighty percent of the parents interviewed said their children's after-school arrangements were different from their own, with several parents emphasizing that these arrangements were "very," "totally," or "completely" different.

When we asked Sandra Hayes whether her mother had been employed full time when she was the same age as her child at the time of the study, she said "I didn't know anyone's mother that was [employed]. Things were totally different. . . . My father worked and my mother stayed home. We got to play under sprinklers and run around the neighborhood." When Albert Rose's live-in girlfriend was a child, "My mother was home, my parents weren't divorced, and we lived in the suburbs. I could easily walk over to my friends' houses." Ruby Nelson pointed out that her single parenthood inevitably makes things different from what she experienced growing up with two parents. She has to work to support her family, and therefore cannot be home during after-school hours.

The respondents described other ways in which their childhoods differed from those of their children. Elizabeth Martell, whose daughter lives in the city, with no siblings close in age, grew up on a farm, where she had the farm to explore, her sisters "to play with or quarrel with," and many chores to do. Pamela Myers grew up in a small town on a lake, Leonard and Rhonda Stiles on a Carribean island. Jane Kelley lived in the country. Valerie Foster spent much of her childhood roaming the woods of West Virginia.

Many parents described the relationships they had with people in their childhood settings as quite different from their family's present relationships to others. Stephanie Samuels said:

> We don't come from this area originally and don't know a lot of people, and there are virtually no other children in the neighborhood so she doesn't have a lot of playmates. This is a sharp contrast to my situation; there were a lot of kids on my block, and we kind of all grew up together.

When Shirley Jackson was a child, "We had the gang to come home with after school. Right after school you went out with your neighborhood friends, playing until dusk." Where the Jacksons live now, there are not many children. Neal Shepard grew up in an urban neighborhood with lots of kids to hang out with. "The only time child care concerned me was when I was sick, someone to be home with me. My view is, the best child care is the peer group."

Rhonda Stiles grew up in Barbados. "It was a small area and everyone knew each other and we looked out for each other. Here I know people by face, but not their character. It's different to bring up kids. Even if I'd come home by myself there was more freedom. [It was] safer." Leonard

Stiles paints a similar picture. "I grew up in a different environment altogether, in the West Indies [Barbados], and everything was different, the climate, the people. There was always someone around to look out for you. If not my mother, then a neighbor or whatever."

Relatives often provided after-school care when parents were employed. In fact, of the 24 parents who reported their own mothers had been employed full time when they were the ages of their children, 10 reported caretaking by grandparents (9 out of 10 were grandmothers, and 5 of the 10 grandparents lived with the respondents). Six mentioned siblings (often sisters), 1 an aunt, and 1 named the "extended family." Three respondents described being watched or cared for by neighbors, and 3 by paid helpers. Several respondents mentioned community programs, classes, or other activities, often in conjunction with supervision by relatives. Two respondents described caring for themselves before their parents returned home.

In three cases, the nature of the parents' work allowed for some parental supervision. Valerie Foster's mother taught at her school, so the mother's working hours coincided with the daughter's school day. Albert Rose's parents both worked at the family's restaurant next door. He describes himself as having been "partly supervised." "We played in the backyard behind the bushes or in our room. . . . [My parents] had people working for them, so they were available if I needed them, but they weren't always around." Similarly, Sharon Cole's parents ran a trailer court out of their home. Sharon "came home, saw Mom and Dad, and played with all the kids in the trailer court." Peter Somers' parents staggered their work hours to allow them to supervise the children more often, but Peter and his siblings were on their own more than his children are now. He was the oldest, so he took care of the younger children when his parents were out.

Two respondents reported their mothers had died before they reached the ages of their children. Sally Robinson was watched by a neighbor after school while her father worked. Emilie Perry was raised by an aunt who "quit nursing to raise my two brothers, three sisters, and me." Her father "went through a lot to keep us," working two jobs throughout Emilie's childhood. An additional respondent, Paula Schapiro, reported that her mother was an alcoholic during her childhood "so she faded in and out of participation in life. . . . When my mom was drunk she was home but not present as an adult, so I was responsible for myself, her, the house, and my younger brother."

Respondents described many ways in which memories of their own childhoods influenced the arrangements they make for their own children. Several said they tried to provide their children with the positive things they themselves had experienced. Pamela Myers was always close to her mother and would like to be close to her own daughter, Rebecca, "but having the time to spend together is a problem." She tries to spend as much time with Rebecca as possible and every third weekend she hires a babysitter for her younger daughter so she and Rebecca can do something special. Tricia Hardy remembers how she felt after a day at school and "how nice it was to be able to come home." She has been sympathetic to her daughter's wish to spend after-school time in her own house. Angela Jones, whose grandmother watched her while her mother worked, noted that her mother had money "for us to be engaged in activities—structured play like art classes, dance classes. I would like that for my kids, but I don't have the money."

Several parents said they tried to improve on their own experiences and rectify things that they had not liked as children. Sally Robinson remembers being very bored sitting in her neighbor's house, and she did not want that for her child. Elaine Shepard always worries that her son will be lonely, "and that does have to do with my childhood. I think I was lonely a lot. I don't think any child should be lonely." Carol Henderson said:

> If I've thought at all about the comparison explicitly I've thought about the isolation I felt being a long way from the town center and school. I've tried to arrange things so Louisa would feel comfortable getting around and spending time with friends. I've tried to choose places to live so that Alan and Louisa can have easy access to school, friends, places to go, things to do. I've encouraged them to spend time with friends, either here or at friends' houses.

Leonard Stiles, who grew up in Barbados, said, "We like it to be different from what we had, because we weren't exposed to much. Looking at the after-school programs, I like him to be exposed to things that I was never exposed to. You know, they go to museums and on trips to other places."

Tonya Latimore's mother

> was always around when I got out of school, and she was very strict with us. Right when we got home, we had to start our homework, and she always had us busy doing something. . . . I found that I do some things similarly to what my mother did, in terms of discipline or punishment,

> but otherwise I try to give them much more freedom than I had when I was their age . . . I try to be less controlling and let them do what they want.

Agnes Banducci echoes this point of view: "My mother wouldn't leave us alone for a minute. . . . We had a traditional Italian family where Mom was home cooking every day." Agnes feels that her mother was always "on top of her," and she wanted more freedom when she was her daughter's age.

Still other parents point to indirect ways in which their own experiences may have influenced their choices for their children, even if they had not been conscious of this at the time. Henry Martell, whose mother never worked and was always home after school, mentioned that one of the reasons they chose an after-school program for their daughter rather than hire a person to come into the house is the high turnover rate, and "I wanted a more stable arrangement for her. So, indirectly, my stable arrangements when I was a child may have affected my decision about Bertha's situation." Paula Schapiro, whose mother was an alcoholic and effectively absent throughout much of her childhood, said she had "never thought of it in terms of what I experienced but I've tried to create a situation in which there's an adult present as a safety net. It takes some of the burden of responsibility off the kids, which I think is appropriate." Emma Lavelle said she did, indirectly, think about her own experiences in planning her son's after-school arrangements. She wanted him to enjoy what he did after school, and as he reached the age at which she herself was involved in the arts, she wanted him to do something creative.

Ironically, one father whose son's after-school arrangement closely matches his own does not believe that he was influenced in his own decisions by childhood experiences. Robert Polansky noted that his grandmother picked him up from school and took care of him, an arrangement similar to the one his son experienced during the first years of the study. However, Robert denied that he had thought about his own childhood experiences when making arrangements for his son. "No . . . it was just logical. I didn't think about my own experiences . . . it was just logical. Why hire a babysitter if my parents are not working and are willing to take care of him?"

Stacey Moore, who says her daughters' mix of structured activities and time on their own is "as close as you could get to a perfect situation," also notes that in allowing her daughters this sort of arrangement she has had to go against her own personal history. "I had to think for a while because it goes against how I was reared where there was always family around and children were never alone. I'd keep [the after-school arrangement] the way it is, but that's because of my children, not because of my instincts."

Jonathan Schapiro had almost the opposite experience, growing up without much supervision and now providing more for his son. Jonathan was very much on his own from the age of 7. "I could bring home friends any time I wanted to, go wherever I wanted to. . . . It seemed perfectly natural to me at the time." Now that he is a father, however, Jonathan believes this pattern "doesn't seem appropriate," and he provides more supervision for his son, Benjamin.

Two thirds of the parents interviewed found their own childhoods provided no guidance as they thought about after-school care for their children. For some, this was a cause of sorrow, whereas others welcomed the changes. Bethany King, whose mother had 15 children and was "always in the house," while Bethany is "never in the house," said that she does not think about her own childhood when making arrangements for her children. "No, I just try and think about what will keep them busy and out of mischief." Stephanie Edwards' childhood experiences "don't seem relevant because the situation is so different." Shirley Jackson believes "the days of trying to make something like what you experienced are gone. I think it's unfortunate." Richard Lynch agrees that "the world has changed." But, he continues, "I see no reason to turn back the clock . . . that's one reason you live where you do—because they have support services for people with this lifestyle [employed parents]."

MAKING DECISIONS

If most parents cannot simply duplicate for their children what they themselves experienced, and many don't want to, on what basis do they make decisions? In choosing after-school arrangements for their children, parents of course consider the child's own needs and desires. Some children prefer sports, others music lessons, and many need time and assistance in completing their homework. For most parents, the child's safety is a paramount concern. Leaving children unsupervised or in the care of strangers often provokes considerable anxiety.

Parents also bring particular values to their decisions about after-school time. One goal of many parents is that after-school time should be productive and should teach new skills. Micah Somers' father believes that "after-school is an extension of learning," and he is pleased that his son is able to accomplish so much during the after-school hours. Bertha Martell's father notes that many activities are available to his daughter at her after-school program, "from piano to computers and drawing and wrestling. But that's not what's important as far as I'm concerned. She goes to school to learn things, but I'm concerned that she has a good time in her after-school program."

Although parents want the best for their children, they often have to consider more than the well-being of the child. Costs set limits on the arrangements many parents can provide. Low-income parents often wish their children could attend karate classes, music lessons, or other specialized activities. Higher income parents who can afford these things often lament their inability to provide a live-in housekeeper or nanny for companionship and supervision in the after-school hours. Parental time and tolerance for chauffering children have their limits, too. The logistics of getting to and from activities can put appealing programs out of reach. Parents worry about children returning home from activities after dark and on foot. Sometimes children are needed by their parents to supervise younger siblings and to take an active part in the running of the household. These responsibilities often conflict with otherwise desirable ways of spending after-school time. Families weigh costs and benefits and strive to promote the well-being of all family members. As David Henderson describes it, "We've tried to balance what everyone's needs in the family are, children and adults, and also what was necessary financially."

EVALUATING SUPERVISED ARRANGEMENTS

Many parents prefer adult supervision for their children, at least in the abstract. Parents often associate adult supervision with "peace of mind," and express satisfaction at the time their children spend in supervised settings. When it comes to evaluating specific embodiments of supervision, however, problems often arise. Parents might have a general wish for a resident adult (apartment-mate, babysitter, housekeeper, au pair, tenant) who could look after the child or provide chauffering and tutoring assistance. Yet, parents often reject such an arrangement because of cost, lack of space in the house, the emotional energy it would take to incorporate another adult into the household, or a belief that the child would not accept the authority of such an adult in any case. Jessica Holden would like "to be able to hire someone that I really felt comfortable and confident in so [my son's] friends could come over, and for help with homework. There probably is someone out there who would do that if you paid them enough."

Many of the parents in the study were cared for after school by their grandmothers or other female relatives when they were growing up. Grandmothers today, however, frequently have jobs themselves (Seligson, 1991). They rarely figure as full time after-school caretakers to the children we interviewed. Gregory Polansky, whose grandparents looked after him for 2 years during our study, is one exception to this rule. Martha Jackson was cared for by her grandmother for 1 year until her grandmother's death, and Marguerite Berger also had 1 year of grandparental after-school care during the course of the study.

More families rely on grandparents intermittently, during school vacations or when children are ill. Irene Castillo's grandmother, who lives down the street from her, takes care of her when Irene is ill or when there is a school vacation. Bertha Martell's grandmother, who also lives nearby, is willing to watch her when she is ill. For 1 year, Jeffrey Wright's grandparents took care of him the day each week his after-school program was closed. George Townsend's grandmother is a school teacher, so she has the same vacation days and can supervise him then. Justin Stiles' grandmother works as a housekeeper, and she has been able to bring Justin to work with her when he is sick. Most employment arrangements, however, are less flexible. Omar Jones would very much like to be with his grandmother after school. "I'd go see my grandmother every day, if she didn't have to work."

Bill MacCarthy turns to his sister to care for his daughters on school vacation weeks. She lives about an hour away and runs a day-care center. Bill drops the girls off with her on Sunday and picks them up on Friday. For single-day holidays, such an arrangement is hardly practical, and the girls spend the day on their own, visiting their father for lunch at midday.

For a time, Mary Ellen Kelliher's mother allowed her two grown daughters to take care of Mary Ellen after school, but Darlene "didn't like some of the things that Mary Ellen was learning from them." One of her daughters showed Mary Ellen photographs of herself giving birth, which Darlene considered inappropriate for her young daughter. Her older daughter is involved in drug use and Darlene does not want her exposed to this.

Families also turn to paid babysitters to supervise children in the after-school hours, yet several parents could not find appropriate sitters and others had bad experiences with babysitters and were leery of relying on them again. Brian Cole's first babysitter quit, and the second proved unreliable, so his mother eventually enrolled him in an after-school program. Irene Castillo's mother could not find an after-school sitter at all and enrolled Irene in an after-school program as a "last resort." The first sitter Bill MacCarthy found slapped his daughter, although more recent sitters, provided by the same agency, have worked out well. Eleanor Townsend tried a babysitter, "but it didn't work out. The boys complained, and the house was a mess." In Jocelyn Williams' view, babysitters cost too much, stay on the phone and sneak their boyfriends in, "and they are no guarantee that things are going to run smoothly. My kids listen to me. Babysitters don't always." The Martells observed their neighbors' experiences with babysitters and were deterred by the rapid turnover in sitters that they saw. They wanted more stability for their own daughter. Stacey Moore would like to have an older teenage girl spend time with her daughters after school, a friend or family member who could take them places if they wanted to explore beyond the confines of the neighborhood. But the young women she would like to hire have active lives of their own, and although willing to babysit occasionally in the evening, are not willing to commit themselves to regular after-school babysitting. Terry Edwards would prefer a "grandmotherly" person to do things with Cynthia after school, but she hasn't found anyone "to fill this role," and money is also a problem.

Several parents discussed their fear of sexual abuse by babysitters who are isolated in the home with the child, and Zack Monroe actually had that nightmare experience. When he was 7 years old he was viciously abused by a babysitter who had been recommended to his mother by the staff of Zack's after-school program. Zack's abuse by a vouched-for babysitter leads one to wonder where, in fact, safety lies.

After-school, extended day, and recreational programs promise stable, structured, and supervised activities in more public settings. Yet they vary enormously and do not always meet children's needs. Some provide engrossing activities and positive peer involvement in the context of thoughtful, consistent adult supervision. Other programs suffer from an unappealing physical setting, high staff turnover, and a dearth of attractive activities. Almost none of the children in the study attended after-school programs in buildings designed initially for this purpose. Many after-school programs met in schools, but could not use regular classroom space. (Nationwide, virtually no before- or after-school program that meets in a school has access to the entire school building; Seppanen, De-Vries, & Seligson, 1993.) Some after-school programs were housed in unappealing and limited basement rooms.

Children sometimes felt unconnected to the other children in the after-school program and parents sometimes regarded other children in the program as bad influences. Peggy Monroe remembers how her son used to come home from the community center crying because some of the other children had beaten him up, and Bernice Gates took her son out of the after-school program he attended because "the other kids were rotten, a bad influence on him." Jason Lehman's parents switched him from one after-school program to another because he "used to come home hurt or crying." He has to take a long bus ride and then cross a busy street to get to his new after-school program, problems that also concern his mother.

Parents debate the merits of particular after-school programs and they weigh different values that could govern the child's use of after-school time. Elizabeth Martell is most pleased that her daughter's after-school program is reliable, stable, and warm, and that there is parental involvement. "Parents have a say even though teachers retain autonomy over what projects to do." Bertha has an "extended group of friends" and "learns to deal with people's mobility—old friends leave, new children and teachers come." Meanwhile, the program is a safe place, a "home base" for Bertha. The problem Elizabeth wrestles with is

> how to judge what they do with their time there. What criterion do you use? What kinds of things does a child need to do? What could you do in that time? What should they push a child to do? You have ambitions for your child. You don't want to waste her time. What's the criterion? Should she be learning or playing?

Elizabeth thinks that some of the activities they have for the children are "trivial," but also that maybe her daughter needs that. Perhaps there could be a little more "learning through play," things like languages, for instance, not in classroom style but more informally. Bertha also loves to swim, and it would be wonderful to incorporate swimming into her after-school program.

Elizabeth notes that Bertha says she would rather be at home after school playing with her parents. But when she is home, she likes to have visits with friends from her after-school program. And when her parents pick her up at the end of the day, she sometimes wants to stay. Parents are most happy with their children's after-school programs when children express their satisfaction in such ways. Elizabeth thinks her daughter would miss the after-school program if she didn't go.

Programs that work well for some children are not so successful for others, either because the children's interests are different, their tolerance for group settings is lower, or they do not fit in as well with the other children present. Derek Linden's mother says that Derek is hyperactive and gets in trouble when he is with other kids. She believes he is "better off alone."

Although after-school and extended day programs are specifically designed to supervise children from the time school ends until 5:45 or 6 p.m., when many parents get home from work, other activities meet during only part of this after-school period. A music lesson or karate class, for instance, might consume only an hour or a half hour sometime between the close of the school day and the early evening. Many children in our study needed to spend unsupervised time if they were going to participate in such activities and there was no adult at home to supervise them in the intervals before or after these activities. (In a survey of more than 12,000 Wisconsin families, J. Steinberg and Riley, 1991, found that children who spent some time in self-care during the week were nearly twice as likely as children using paid child-care arrangements to participate in sports, clubs, or lessons after school.) Activities tended to cost more per hour than extended day programs, yet they were popular with children, who enjoyed choosing something that satisfied their own particular interests.

Nine-year-old Micah Somers uses the after-school hours intensively to learn new skills he has chosen himself. He plays soccer twice a week (and other sports in their seasons), has a tap dancing class once a week, and takes Suzuki piano lessons once a week, in addition to the saxophone lessons he takes at school. After school he also spends time at home doing homework and practicing his instruments. Even with all these responsibilities, he finds some time to get together with friends, often at the large school field at the end of his street. Although his mother's irregular work schedule sometimes allows her to drive him to these commitments, Micah is learning how to get where he needs to go on foot or using public transportation or taxis. The variety and extent of his activities would be impossible for Micah if his parents did not also grant him the freedom of time on his own before and after these activities.

Although most parents move their children away from adult-supervised after-school arrangements with concern and even regret, several parents in the study express reservations about keeping children in adult-supervised settings. Jane Kelley says she has "lots of problems with kids in extended day care" and thinks it is doing strange things to children, making them needy and immature because they are always being "attended to" in some structured way, rather than having free time or alone time at home. Jocelyn Williams thinks that after-school programs are good for children, "but only up to a point. Some kids are 14 years old and still in a program. That's ridiculous." As she sees it, "kids are better off on their own. Kids can cope. It's the parents who can't cope."

Evan Delaney's parents, who are divorced and share custody, are generally satisfied with their son's after-school program. Yet they believe that as a result of the time he has spent in supervised and structured settings after school he has not developed the skills of initiating social contacts and activities on his own, skills that come more readily to children who must seek out their own friends and things to do, rather than having these experiences provided for them. Evan's parents have begun allowing him to come home 1 day a week in order to develop such skills, and to prepare for spending more unstructured and unsupervised time on his own in the future. Yvonne Hayes' mother similarly initiates some unsupervised time for Yvonne in the final year of the study as "practice" for the following year, when Yvonne will be unsupervised all afternoon.

A family may reject otherwise attractive after-school arrangements for reasons that are idiosyncratic, yet extremely important to the family concerned. Derek Linden's mother, for instance, is anxious about any after-school alternative that requires Derek or his younger brother to travel without her from one location to another. Her sons have twice been kidnapped by her ex-husband, and she resists exposing them to situations in which they would be vulnerable to yet another attempt. Less dramatically, Stephanie Samuels is distressed when snacks like ice cream and lasagna are served at her daughter, Julie's after-school program. Although many children and parents might welcome such treats, Julie has a weight problem that can only be exacerbated by such fattening foods.

SEMISUPERVISION

Some children have after-school arrangements that are difficult to characterize as either supervised or unsupervised. Seven-year-old Meiguei Chen spends several hours each day after school in the children's room of the town's public library. The librarians have no official responsibility for her, but they are aware of her presence and take an interest in her well-being. Earlier she had briefly attended an after-school program, but she didn't like it. According to her mother, "we lived near the library and she's always enjoyed coming here, so we decided to try it."

What Meiguei likes best about going to the library after school is that "it's quiet, and they have grown-ups here when I need them." She explains that the librarians give you a star for each book you read, but because Meiguei reads so many books, she only gets a star for every two books she reads. Reading is one of the things Meiguei thinks she is getting better at because she is on her own at the library after school. What she does not like is "that I don't see many friends, and that I'm bored sometimes and that I'm not allowed to go to the park." She thinks the way she spends her time after school is "okay," but she would prefer to have a babysitter. Yet there do not seem to be many alternatives. "This is the only thing I can do. I don't like after-school. My mother can't find a babysitter."

When asked about her experiences the day of the interview, Meiguei describes taking the bus from her school to the library, reading some books, then asking the librarians for two stars. Next Meiguei went to the toddlers' room and watched the movie. ("I already saw it. It was kind of boring.") Then she checked if she had a dime "to call my mother to ask if I could wear short sleeves tomorrow, but I didn't have a dime." After that, Meiguei sat outside for a while. One of her friends came. "She brought something for me to eat. She had the chicken pox. At first I ran away. Then I remembered I already had the chicken pox." After this friend left, Meiguei just sat outside and almost fell asleep. A whole class of preschoolers came by. She went inside and read more books and looked for books to take out but couldn't find any. Finally, she came back in and took a short nap. "When I woke up I waited for my mother." Meiguei mentions that a friend used to take violin lessons nearby and would come to the library first and visit with Meiguei. Now she rarely does.

Meiguei's mother, Weining, has misgivings about the arrangement and would prefer that Meiguei attend an after-school program.

> I would feel more comfortable with someone watching her. . . . Sometimes she leaves the library and goes outside to play. She just plays right outside the library, but I worry. She's too young to be by herself. You hear about children being kidnapped and you worry.

But Weining believes that Meiguei likes the library very much:

> She even comes here on Saturdays. . . .She doesn't even want to go to summer camp. She cried when I told her about it. But she knows there is no choice. The library will close for vacation. . . . I keep trying to get her to go to an after-school program, but Meiguei doesn't want to go.

The library director has told Meiguei that they are no longer going to allow children under 8 years of age in the library without their parents, but that they like Meiguei and will make an exception for her.

When 8-year-old Cynthia Edwards gets home from school her mother is generally there, but she is also generally asleep because she works the midnight shift as a medical technologist. Terry Edwards works the night shift because it offers more money and because she believes that leaving Cynthia alone while she is asleep at night is preferable to leaving her alone during the day. Terry's work schedule allows her at least to be physically present in the afternoon, although it also requires that her children be alone throughout the night.

Cynthia knows not to wake her mother unless there is an emergency. (If something did come up Cynthia says she would "wake Mom up. Pounce on her.") She is careful to bring her key with her to school so that she can let herself into the apartment without disturbing her mother, and she avoids noisy activities like playing the piano that might wake her mother during the afternoon.

Terry cannot afford an after-school program. She considered leaving Cynthia in the care of her older brother, Craig, who is 15. But, she says, Craig was "having his own problems" and wasn't able to take care of Cynthia. For a while Craig was supposed to pick Cynthia up at the end of the school day and walk her home, but he was "not responsible enough to consistently get there on time." Terry recently found an older girl from the neighborhood whom she pays to walk Cynthia home from school. Craig does sometimes take Cynthia to the library.

When Terry is working at night she can sometimes drop in to see Cynthia and her brother. "It's not terribly easy, but I can." She estimates she has done so about five times in the last year. These trips home are "not to visit, because she's sleeping. But just to make sure they're all right. Just to reassure myself." Terry sees these trips as "mostly for me, because they don't know I've been there."

In later years of the study, Terry arranges for Cynthia to have activities after school several days a week. Cynthia enjoys these activities, and they also make it possible for Terry to have a more reasonable amount of sleep. "The days she has activities after school, it's great. I've been out working the night before and I can sleep later and not worry. Trying to get even 6 hours asleep before I go back is difficult sometimes."

Terry believes that Cynthia is "very happy" with the new arrangements, "although maybe that's wishful thinking." At the programs she attends Cynthia is learning new skills. "She has awake people with her, instead of an unconscious mother!" Terry believes Cynthia "enjoys the company, the structure of these programs. She's a curious little girl. She likes to learn. And I think she likes the variety."

Terry would prefer her daughter to have a more substantial and regular after-school program:

> I would like to have her in a program that is structured, varied, and specifically directed to the interests of that age group, that didn't cost too much. That would help the isolation problem and my sleeping problem.

Terry considers herself reasonably satisfied with her daughter's after-school arrangements: "I feel more comfortable now than I did a couple of years ago. I think that's because I'm getting used to it. It's working. It's not great, but we're getting by."

Cynthia's preferred arrangement after school would be to go to her school's after-school program or to a friend's house. She understands, however, that the after-school program costs too much, and she appreciates why her mother wants her in her own home after school. But Cynthia thinks that some of her friends have more fun than she does after school "because they go to [the after-school program] or a friend's house. At the program they play or do whatever they want. They can have a snack, go outside, and play till Mom picks them up." Cynthia says she knows her mother needs to work. "I know that much. I wish she could just go outside and pick money off the trees."

In the final year of the study, Terry switches to the day shift so she can spend nights at home. Sometimes Cynthia even meets her mother at work so they can walk home together. Cynthia is very pleased with the new arrangement: "I think it's a lot better now. She used to work at night and sleep all day. That didn't work at all. Now I'm more confident, although I'm still half scared of the dark."

At 14 years of age, Gregory Polansky has an after-school job 2 or 3 days a week, but spends most of his after-school time hanging out with friends, usually at fast food restaurants or walking around the streets of the town. At his home, meanwhile, the middle-aged woman who lives with his family looks after Gregory's 2-year-old brother. Having a live-in nanny or babysitter is a favorite wish of many parents in the study. But in the Polansky household the live-in babysitter is seen as solely devoted to Gregory's younger brother. She has no responsibility for Gregory, and Gregory is not accountable to her. Gregory's father, Robert, says that even if the babysitter is in the house, Gregory isn't "with" her. Gregory's mother, Claire, says she doesn't like Gregory to bring friends home "because the baby gets too excited and it's hard for the babysitter."

What Claire likes least about Gregory's after-school arrangements is his "hanging out. I don't know what could be done about that. I have no choice. I guess they need to spend time with friends at this age." She notes that there are no recreational activities in the town for kids after school. Unless someone can drive the kids to the roller skating rink they can't get anywhere. Claire believes that what Gregory likes best about his after-school arrangements is the freedom he experiences. What he likes least, she believes, is "for us to tell him when to be home. Sometimes he makes up stories to explain why he's late." Robert says he doesn't think there is anything "best" about his son's after-school arrangements, although there is one advantage, at least, to having the nanny at home. "He can't bring friends around and go crazy."

Gregory says that he does not really enjoy the time he spends hanging out with friends in the town. He says the town is boring, and that there is not much to do. If he had a choice he would move to a different city with more things to do. "If there was somewhere to go, I'd do that. All there is here is a bowling alley that no one goes to."

In emergencies and at some other times, Meiguei Chen, Cynthia Edwards, and Gregory Polansky have adults available to them in the after-school hours: Meiguei has the librarians, Cynthia her mother, and Gregory his brother's live-in babysitter. But for most of their after-school time they seem more unsupervised than supervised, unconnected to adults, and responsible for themselves.

SPECIAL ISSUES FOR LOW-INCOME FAMILIES

Low-income parents face particular difficulties in finding acceptable after-school arrangements. Frequently, they cannot afford the activities their children desire or cannot arrange their children's transportation home from these programs. Most do not own cars and many live in neighborhoods poorly served by public transportation. These neighborhoods are often dangerous as well, limiting the options their children enjoy for outdoor play. Stanley Gates, for instance, is 15 years old and on his own most school day afternoons. His mother permits him to leave the house, but because of the dangerousness of the neighborhood he must stay right in front of their building, or at least go no further than either corner of the street. Stanley spends most of his time indoors watching television and playing video games. In contrast, many much younger children in safer neighborhoods are allowed to explore their own communities by bicycle and on foot.

Many poor parents work nonstandard shifts, either to earn higher hourly wages or because this is when the work is available. Some work more than one full time job because the hourly pay for their work is so low. Such parental schedules mean that most after-school programs, even if they were otherwise accessible, would not provide coverage during all the hours the parent is absent. In low-income and especially single-parent families, children's labor may be needed for sibling caretaking and housework, restricting other options.

The Jones family lives in public housing and both parents work to support themselves and their three children. Like one out of every three employed couples with children (Presser, 1986), these parents have arranged to work different shifts so that one of them can be home when the other is at work. The family does not own a car. When their oldest child, Omar, was younger he regularly attended the after-school program in their housing project or he waited in the hallway for a parent to come home from work. These days, his mother, Angela, is often with him until his father comes home, but several times a week she must leave for work about 1 hour before Mr. Jones returns from his job. On these occasions, 8-year-old Omar is responsible for his 4-year-old brother, Christopher, and his 14-month-old sister, Jamila. According to Angela, the rules are clear. "I don't allow the kids to touch the appliances. They have to stay in one room. The rest of the house is closed off. If Christopher has to go to the bathroom, Omar has to take him. Jamila is supposed to stay in the playpen." Furthermore, Omar knows that no one else should be allowed to learn that he is home alone with his siblings. When he is in charge at home, Omar cannot call or see other people except in an emergency. Even Angela's mother does not know that Omar is watching the other children. "If she did, she wouldn't approve."

According to Angela there were really no other possible arrangements she could make. Her own mother works full time, and Angela says, "I don't like anyone else watching the kids. I don't trust other people with the kids, and I fear sexual abuse." Yet Angela feels bad that so much responsibility is being placed on her son, and does not feel that what they are doing is right. "By law, Omar is too young to watch the kids. Something could happen and we'd feel terrible. Maybe someday I won't have to depend on my son."

The advantage of this arrangement, according to Angela, is that "I'm not late for work. I can leave on time. It keeps me from losing my job." She also feels good that she can trust her son. "He follows my directions. He doesn't tell people he's watching his siblings. He knows what goes on in here stays in here. We are a family. We keep our business in our house." She also hears only good things about Omar from her friends and neighbors. Omar is "a respected little boy in the neighborhood."

But Angela is very unhappy about the arrangement. Omar "doesn't have the freedom he should after school. School can be a pressure and then he has the added responsibility of watching his siblings. I'm surprised he's not doing badly in school." She sees no benefits to Omar's spending time with his brother and sister because they don't like it and they fight often. "Christopher doesn't like being bossed around by Omar." Although Omar may be gaining a little in self-reliance or self-confidence, "it's too much responsibility for him. It may hurt him some day. If I had a better job I wouldn't have to put him through this." When asked how she thinks her son feels about the arrangement, Angela says, "He's hurt about it. He cries, 'Mommy, when are you going to stop so I can go out and play?'. It's only normal to feel bad when your mother lays so much responsibility on you." Angela thinks Omar dislikes the arrangement very much and would prefer to go to an after-school program, play outside with friends, and take karate and piano lessons. Angela would also prefer different after-school arrangements for Omar. When asked about the obstacles that prevent her from having such arrangements she says, simply, "Money." Angela rates Omar's after-school arrangement as the most stressful realm of her life, and hopes one day she can change it. "Some day I would like not to lean on Omar like I do now."

Ten days before our second interview with the family, Angela Jones left her job, accepting a tremendous cut in family income as the price of making more time available to be with her children.

When Jocelyn Williams was growing up, her parents both worked full time, but only at one job each. According to Jocelyn, life is tougher now, and you need to work more than one job to survive. Jocelyn separated from her husband some months prior to the study. She is currently working two full-time jobs and says she would work four jobs if her schedule allowed it. "You're going to die anyway. It might as well be from hard work." When Jocelyn was growing up, her brother watched her in the afternoons before her parents came home from work. "But he often left me. He knew I could take care of myself." Jocelyn now has a son, Andrew, who is 13 and a daughter, Layla, who is 11, and she has made very sure that they too know how to take care of themselves.

Jocelyn works as a senior office assistant from early morning to late evening on weekdays, arriving home around 10 p.m. Without education beyond high school, Jocelyn's pay is low. Working two jobs allows her to approach a middle-class lifestyle. She is currently looking for a third, weekend job, as she is trying to save money for a house.

Jocelyn's hard work provides her children with advantages and opportunities they otherwise would not have, including residence in a pleasant apartment building in a middle-class neighborhood. Jocelyn also models the kind of devotion to hard work she would like to see in her children, and her work-impelled absence forces them to develop the self-reliance that Jocelyn values so highly.

With Jocelyn away most of their waking hours, her children have had to learn to take care of themselves. They sometimes drop in at the after-school and vacation program in their apartment building, but they take care of themselves most afternoons and evenings, and most of the time on school vacation days and in the summer. On the one hand, Jocelyn says, "no kid should be alone that much. It's not fair." Yet, on the other hand, kids need to learn how to take care of themselves because life will demand it of them anyway. Jocelyn does not take time off from work to be with Layla when she is sick. "I have a good record. I don't take time off when I'm sick. I'll buy everything she needs ahead of time. Sometimes I feel bad, but she has to learn to take care of herself."

Jocelyn points to ways her children benefit from their after-school arrangements. "The fact that they know they can take care of themselves. They feel good about it. It makes them feel grown-up. They enjoy the freedom they have." Jocelyn benefits as well from knowing that her children can take care of themselves, that she can have "trust and faith" in them. "It's reassuring to know that when I work I don't have to worry."

Although Jocelyn is enthusiastic about her children's after-school arrangement ("I love it, I really do"), she also says that if she could find a program that offered technical knowledge and provided transportation home, she would enroll them in it. But, she says, they do not have programs like that, and transportation to and from any program remains a problem. She also raised the issue of how parents, especially single parents, are going to deal with after-school arrangements in the future. "How are they going to cope? What are we going to do as a society to help? We need more programs—educational—something meaningful. The schools don't do enough." In a later interview, Jocelyn comments that both her daughter and her son would like to attend a program that really utilizes their talents, a program where they could meet new friends. Jocelyn would like to see her daughter in a program "where she can realize her abilities. . . . I'd like to see her in a program that will help her in the future. . . . What she does is fine, but there's so much she could do." But programs like this that also provide reliable transportation home do not exist, and Jocelyn is not able to escort her children home in the late afternoon.

Emilie Perry has a high school education and works as a data entry operator. She gets home at 5:30 p.m., 3 hours later than her 10-year-old daughter Jasmin. According to Emilie:

> Jasmin comes right home after school and calls me right away. What she does after that varies from day to day. Monday she is free until 5 p.m. when she has track practice. Tuesdays and Thursdays she has no structured activities. Wednesday she goes back to school for her jazz class at 3 p.m. Class lasts until 4 p.m., after which she comes back home. Friday she is free until she picks up her younger brother [Leon] at 5 p.m. and watches him until I [her mother] return.

Emilie regrets her absence during the day.

> I would prefer to be home with both my kids. They miss out on a lot because I'm not here. Like there is a reading lab at [the university] I'd like

to go to because she has reading problems, but I have no way to provide her transportation. I worry about safety. I'd blame myself if anything happened to her.

As Emilie sees it, "the only other alternative is to stay home and be on welfare. I was on welfare the first 3 months after Jasmin was born, and I hated it. They ran my life. I hated it. I'm used to working." As she says at another point, "I work for selfish reasons."

Although Emilie hopes that Jasmin's after-school arrangements are teaching her to be responsible and giving her a feeling of independence, Emilie's preferred arrangements for Jasmin would be "totally different." Emilie says, "she shouldn't have to take care of another child." The obstacles that prevent Emilie from realizing a different arrangement are "economic. No money. No other way." Emilie says that she has told Jasmin, "I could stay home and collect welfare or I can work. She understands that. She doesn't mind minding him [Leon], but sometimes he aggravates her."

When Bernice Gates was a child her mother was always home. As Bernice says, "with 12 kids she had to be." Bernice completed 2 years of college, got married, and had four children. Her husband left the household shortly before the study began, leaving Bernice to meet the mortgage payments and support the family. In the first year of the study she worked from 8:30 a.m. to 4 p.m. on weekdays in a clerical position and again from 5 p.m. to midnight on Thursdays in a human services job dealing with retarded adults.

Stanley, her youngest child, is 12, and he is on his own for less than 1 hour after school every day but Thursday, when he goes to a tutor and then accompanies his mother to her evening job. In previous years, Stanley attended an after-school program, but, she says, the kids there were "rotten" and were a bad influence on him. At other times, his older sister and brothers have watched Stanley or Bernice or her ex-husband has been home.

Bernice does not like the fact that Stanley is home by himself because of the dangerous neighborhood in which they live, and because Stanley is a "devil" himself. She worries a lot. "Is he going to be all right?" She signals when she telephones (letting the phone ring three times, hanging up, then calling again) allowing him to avoid speaking to other phone callers, including his father, whom he does not want to talk to, and preventing him from letting others know he is home alone. Stanley never complains, "except about being bored, which is a daily complaint." In the past he took karate, but that didn't last, and swimming, but that didn't last either. Half the time the pool was closed and he became very discouraged. Now he wants to take tennis, but Bernice does not think she can afford the lessons.

In the second year of the study, Bernice has kept her day job and expanded her evening job to every weekday evening and Saturday mornings. She takes Stanley with her to her second job on Monday and they do something special together. Bernice says that she began taking Stanley with her because of "guilt on my part. I feel like he needs more attention. I didn't work full time when the other kids were growing up. I certainly didn't have two jobs." It also bothers Bernice that Stanley is not doing anything constructive during his after-school time. Nor is she confident that he follows her rules. Stanley is supposed to come right home after school and stay there until Bernice calls him or he calls her to ask her permission to go out, but when Bernice calls, Stanley is rarely home. She would prefer that he attend an after-school program, but he has refused, and she says that if she insisted, she knows he would "act out."

In the following year, Bernice continues at her two jobs and Stanley again spends time unsupervised at home. Bernice believes that he is still not making productive use of his time after school, and she also does not like Stanley's friends. "A couple of them are good kids, but most of them are trouble." Bernice would prefer Stanley to be in a structured program, perhaps one focused on sports. "I think the ideal would be a program that provided him with tutoring. But that is impossible because he doesn't like doing homework as it is and so he would rebel and become defiant." Bernice says she feels guilty leaving Stanley at home so much alone.

> It is hard for me to let go because he is the baby. Yet I know I have to work. I worry constantly. Every night I wish he were with me. I am always wondering, "What is he doing now?" I feel I am neglecting him, cheating him, because I did so much with my other children.

Bernice used to bring Stanley with her to her evening job.

> He used to come with me constantly. I'm free to bring him along. He doesn't go with me much this year, partly because he is getting older, and partly because, one night, when he was with me, one of the residents spat at him. He said he understood, they're retarded, but I know it bothers him still.

In the final year of the study, Bernice quit her evening job to spend more time with Stanley. She works until 4 p.m. and gets home by 4:15 p.m. Stanley is home a bit before her, but now he usually leaves for the recreation center with his friends by 3 or 3:30 p.m., and does not return home until 9 or 9:30 p.m. By the time Bernice gets home, he is gone. The "one good thing" about this arrangement "is that he is not hanging out on the street with a bad crowd. I do know where he's at, and that gives me a sense of relief." Bernice would prefer for Stanley to be involved in "some kind of educational program rather than just activities, maybe half and half." Yet this would be "a waste of my time and money because his interest is not there. His interest is in the streets and money, in having fun."

Darlene Kelliher works only one full-time job, although her schedule includes regular work in the evenings and on weekends. She is home on two weekdays. Mary Ellen, Darlene's only child remaining at home, attends the after-school program in the housing project where they live, and then goes to a licensed foster care parent (Mrs. DeVito) who takes care of her until Darlene returns from work, usually at about 8:30 p.m. Although Darlene trusts the after-school program, and Mrs. DeVito is a close friend, other dangers in the housing project environment worry her. Throughout the 4 years of the study, Darlene expressed her concern about Mary Ellen's exposure to drugs and young prostitutes. Apparently, Darlene's older daughters succumbed to such dangers. Without the higher income that a second job would provide, Darlene and Mary Ellen are in the housing project to stay.

Parents whose earning power is limited have distinctive problems in arranging appropriate after-school care for their children. To earn enough to support their families, many work more than one job, often arriving home in the late evening and even spending time at work on the weekends. After-school programs that close by 6 p.m. and do not operate on weekends assume a standard work week. These programs do not begin to provide adequate supervision for children whose parents work much longer hours or those whose work schedules (even for a 40-hour work week) extend into the evening and weekend. Dangerous neighborhoods in which children may be victimized by crime or may themselves be lured into criminal activity make unsupervised time at home far more hazardous than it is in safer areas of the city. Low-income parents are also unlikely to be able to afford the activities they would like for their children or to be able to provide their children with safe transportation to and from such activities.

Low-income parents must weigh their children's need for supervision and parental attention against their children's need for economic support (including residence in a relatively safe community). Often, there is no truly acceptable solution to this dilemma, and parents must live with the realization that their children are endangered.

MAKING AFTER-SCHOOL WORK

Deciding on children's after-school arrangements, doing the registering, chauffering, telephoning, and other logistical support to make it work, and responding to cancellations and other crises, is no trivial responsibility. Many parents devote considerable energy to facilitating this part of the child's day.

Parents often rearrange their work lives to accommodate their children's after-school needs, in some instances changing careers to be more available to their children. Emma Lavelle switched to her current job because "it had a school schedule" and did not produce "pressures to take home with me." Jane Kelley used to work as a nurse at the university level, but moved to the public school system "for the hours and the vacations." Tricia Hardy left nursing for teaching (which required going back to school) so that her work schedule would allow her more time with her daughter. According to her husband, Laura Somers could get a full-time job that she might enjoy more than her current combination of part-time positions, but she sticks to her flexible set of part-time jobs because "she wants to be there for the kids." Elizabeth Martell went to law school right after her daughter, Bertha, was born, but she became discouraged about the long hours involved. "I knew it wouldn't get any better once I was a lawyer, so I quit. At the same time, though, I had become interested in the work I'm doing." She has pursued a successful academic career, yet even in this second career she has put her daughter's needs first, limiting the time she spends away from home. If she had had other priorities, her husband says, she would probably be dean of her university by now.

In single-parent households, after-school responsibilities fall on the shoulders of the solo parent, sometimes requiring major readjustments in the parent's work life. One fourth of the single parents we interviewed reported they had chosen a career with shorter or more flexible work hours to accommodate their children's after-school needs. (None of the single parents, however, said they had forgone a career advance to accommodate the child's after-school needs, perhaps because the parent's income from employment was also of heightened importance in single-parent households.) In households with one parent, children often share household responsibilities such as meal preparation and the care of younger siblings.

Two-parent households allow adults to share responsibility for the child's after-school needs or to create a division of labor in which one parent takes on that responsibility. Among the two-parent households in this study, about one third displayed virtually equal involvement in facilitating the child's after-school arrangements, whereas in two thirds of the two-parent families, one parent was clearly the after-school "specialist." In our study, all such after-school specialists were mothers. The Hendersons are representative of the minority of two-parent families in which both parents share equally in the child's after-school arrangements. Both have chosen work that is convenient to their home, and both parents call their daughter, Louisa, after school and receive calls and visits at work from her.

The Shepards are representative of the larger group of two-parent families in which there is an after-school specialist. Elaine Shepard, who chose a career with shorter and more flexible work hours and work that is convenient to home in order to accommodate her son's after-school needs, chauffeurs him to various activities after school, calls him and visits him during the after-school hours. Neal Shepard receives after-school telephone calls from his son, but is otherwise not involved in the day-to-day business of his son's after-school arrangements.

Even in families in which parents divide the after-school tasks equally, mothers often function as supervisors, keeping track of changing schedules and alerting fathers to their responsibilities from day to day. Jonathan Schapiro performs as many after-school tasks on a daily basis as his wife does, but when we asked him about his child's previous after-school arrangements, he said that he did not remember what the past arrangements had been and suggested we ask his wife. As he explained, his wife "takes responsibility for that part of the family." In the Somers family, both parents assist their children in the after-school hours, driving them to a wide variety of activities. Yet, according to both parents, Micah's mother, Laura, is the one responsible for orchestrating the complicated weekly after-school plans for the family. Micah's father, Peter, says he gets involved in the children's after-school arrangements "kicking and screaming," but then finds his involvement very satisfying. When Laura was out of town briefly, "we survived beautifully. I was the number one parent." Peter says, "I'm happier the more I'm involved."

Disputes over the division of parental responsibility for children's after-school arrangements can became acrimonious, particularly when one spouse's perceived failure to help out endangers the other's job. Angela Jones says that being a parent has created problems for her in almost every job she has had.

> There are almost always problems. The kids are sick or the arrangements you made aren't working out. They get tired of hearing it. I've had some jobs I've really liked but have ended up leaving because of things that came up with the kids. That's why I'm always after [my husband] to do more, to be more responsible as far as the kids go.

Angela resents what she sees as her husband's abdication of responsibility for the children's welfare when this conflicts with his work.

> He is so into his job. It is up to me to make sure [the kids] are safe. Those are my decisions as far as he is concerned. . . . I've tried to make him understand the responsibility shouldn't always fall on the mother. Why should I always have to mess up things at my job?

In contrast to married parents, divorced parents who share custody of a child and maintain two separate households for the child tend to take a more equal share of responsibility for the after-school arrangements. In shared custody households, fathers are as likely as mothers to call the child after school, receive calls from the child, visit the child, and chauffeur the child to activities. Three of the five joint custody fathers in our study reported they had foregone career advances because of their child's after-school needs or had chosen a career with shorter or more flexible work hours, whereas none of the fathers in two-parent families reported such accommodations in their work lives. Certainly, the demands of shared custody arrangements put stronger pressures on fathers to assume responsibility for their children's lives in the after-school hours. It could also be that fathers who choose joint custody, sometimes making great efforts to maintain their own households within walking distance of those of their ex-wives, and within the same school district, are men who are highly motivated to maintain extensive involvement in the day-to-day lives of their children.

This study suggests that children's after-school needs have a substantial impact on the work lives of their parents, particularly their mothers. The findings are convergent with Riley's (1997) study of after-school child-care needs in Milwaukee, Wisconsin. Riley found that 26% of parents in two-parent families and 34% of single parents reported that the lack of good child care kept them or their spouses from working the number of hours they would prefer. Similarly, Seligson, Fersh, Marshall, and

Marx (1990) found that the lack of high-quality, affordable after-school care is a substantial barrier to the employment and training of many parents. In their study, almost one third of the low-income mothers who were not in school or training said they would enter training or school if they could find acceptable after-school care for their children. Almost half of the nonemployed women from moderate income families said they would seek jobs if affordable, high-quality after-school care were available.

THE CHILD'S PERSPECTIVE

As parents try to promote the well-being of the child while attending to the needs of other family members and the limitations of the family budget, children have their own agendas. According to Medrich et al. (1982), the activities preadolescents prefer are informal and unstructured, maximize freedom, cost money, and are done with friends. These preferences conflict with those of parents, who tend to prefer safe, supervised, and goal-directed activities for their children. Confirming Medrich et al.'s insights, children in our study often expressed the wish to "veg out" after a grueling day in school, to spend after-school time with specific friends, and to engage in activities such as karate or dancing classes that cost money. They often resisted their parents' efforts to keep them in adult-supervised arrangements, even those they had enjoyed as younger children. Television holds great attraction for many children, but parents generally regard it as a useless or destructive pastime.

Children's desire for spontaneity and freedom works against their acceptance of after-school and extended day programs, and such sentiments tend to intensify as children get older. Diana Hardy says that the best thing about being on her own after school is,

> I get more my own choices . . . what I wanna do. Compared to after-school, [which] was just like school. You had a choice of a few things and if you didn't do one you sat in a corner. [Being on my own] gives me more time to myself.

Eric Holden contrasts the activities that were available to him at his after-school program with the absence of activities in his current unsupervised arrangement at home:

> Sometimes I feel like going to an after-school program. But when I go I don't like the set-up. . . . I'd like to go swimming or something. I don't like having to go. I want to be able to go.

Eric would like the opportunity to go swimming spontaneously, when he feels like it, but he rejects an arrangement in which swimming is regularly mandated for him.

From the child's perspective, one of the most serious and frequent problems with after-school time is not being able to be with close friends. Friends might attend school together, but one might stay on at the after-school program, while the other returns home. One child unsupervised at home might be allowed to have friends visit, but the child's close friends might live too far away to come, or their parents might prohibit their visiting an unsupervised friend. Children who attend schools outside their own neighborhoods are particularly likely to have difficulties seeing friends from school (if they return home after school) or friends from the neighborhood (if they stay on at the school's after-school program). Although children can often have contact with same-age peers after school, many children find themselves separated from their own particular friends during the after-school hours. When we asked children what kind of after-school arrangement they would prefer if given the choice, the majority told us they would go to a friend's house. The move to self-care was often designed, in part, to make it easier for children to get together with good friends, echoing J. Steinberg and Riley's (1991) finding that children who spend some time in self-care are much more likely to go to friends' houses after school on a regular basis than are children using paid child care after school.

Although their parents' work schedules make this difficult or impossible, many children, particularly the younger ones, also wish for more contact with their parents in the after-school hours. Children often want to see their parents, talk to them, and have physical closeness with them during this time. Several children are able to visit parents at work and relish doing so, whereas others content themselves with telephone calls, and still others cannot see or talk with their parents until they return from work. Although caring attention from other adults is appreciated, and although children often enjoy the freedom of time on their own, many still wish they could have more time with their own parents after school.

A DELICATE BALANCE

Finding and sustaining acceptable after-school arrangements is often a complicated, subtle, and time-consuming process, requiring the negotiation of agreements between family members with conflicting agendas. Generally with limited options, parents seek out arrangements they believe will work best for their families.

5

Changes in After-School Arrangements Over Time

Julie Samuels attended an after-school program every day of the week when we first interviewed her at age 8, and her mother, Stephanie, felt positive about it:

> I don't worry about her. I know she likes her teachers, and I've been pleased by some of the activities they've come up with. . . . There are times when I go to pick her up and she's not ready to go, and that's nice, that she's that caught up in her projects.

Also, the program gives Julie a chance to complete her homework. "By the time I pick her up, it's 6, and that's a long day for an 8-year-old, so it's nice that at least she can get her homework out of the way." On the other hand, the physical environment of the program leaves something to be desired:

> The kids are stuck in basement rooms that frankly aren't very clean. . . . There are also times when I wonder if the children are sometimes undersu-

> pervised. I don't fault the teachers . . . I think they are doing their best at a difficult job, but they are understaffed, and I have seen kids waiting in hallways unsupervised.

Julie confirms her mother's perception that she likes her after-school program "somewhat." She enjoys being in the "big kids' room" this year, compared to where she was in the previous year, but she says there is hardly anything to do at the program. She says that she has thought of more activities for the teacher, and sometimes they have done them. She most likes free time and group time, when all the "big kids" gather around and discuss things, but she would prefer to go to a friend's house after school.

In the second year of the study, Julie was still attending the after-school program every day, but Stephanie was not as pleased. A whole new staff has been hired and she believes they are not as good or as motivated as those the previous year. There are also some disruptive children whose parents are at home but who do not want their children at home because they are difficult. "The teachers are having a tough time and the parents aren't backing the teachers." Stephanie says that Julie is often alone and not included in any activities, and the staff does nothing about this. Sometimes they do not know where Julie is. The quality of snacks has also deteriorated, according to Stephanie. There is less fruit, more fattening foods such as ice cream and lasagna, and Julie already has a weight problem.

By the third year of the study, Julie has left the after-school program and is spending weekday afternoons without adult supervision. On Mondays and Wednesdays she comes home on the school bus and spends time alone until Stephanie gets home. On Tuesdays and Fridays she walks from school to a girlfriend's house and plays there. This friend's mother also works, but there is an older sibling in the apartment and grandparents on another floor of the triple decker. On Thursdays, one of Julie's classmates takes the bus home and plays with her.

Stephanie is enthusiastic about the days Julie goes to her friend Amy's house. Amy has a yard and an extra bicycle. They live right by the school and can use the school playground. She even has a cat Julie can cuddle, and grandparents in the house. Stephanie also believes that Amy is "the most lovely, giving child." Having Julie at Amy's gives Stephanie "peace of mind." Stephanie also suspects that Julie enjoys the "tempered independence" she has there, with the assurance that adults are not too far away, if she needs anything. Stephanie wishes Julie did not have to be home alone two afternoons a week. "She does okay, but there've been times she's told me she's lonely. In bad weather, when I'm late getting home, she worries. It's probably less of a worry if you have someone with you." Still, Stephanie believes that Julie's new arrangements represent "a world of difference" to what she had before, and that the change is positive.

Most after-school research has been cross-sectional, assessing a child's experiences at one point in time. When children's after-school arrangements are examined over a multiyear period, change over time is far more typical than stability. Most children move from primarily supervised to primarily unsupervised settings, although some also move in the other direction, toward greater adult supervision in the after-school hours.

BECOMING UNSUPERVISED

At the beginning of our study, adult supervision was the norm for most of the children, most of the time. Children spent their after-school hours in formal programs, in specialized activities such as team practices and music lessons, and at home with adult caretakers such as relatives or paid babysitters. Over the course of the study, more and more children ventured into unsupervised settings, until by the end of the study all but three of the children were regularly spending some unsupervised time each week. (In one family the mother was no longer employed, and in the other two families the children continued to attend formal after-school programs.)

Children typically began spending unsupervised time at age 10 or 11, although one fourth of the children in the study were unsupervised at a younger age. These figures are in accord with those of a survey of midwestern families (J. Steinberg & Riley, n.d.) that found that three quarters of the surveyed parents believed that most children were ready for regular self-care between the ages of 10 and 12. Furthermore, these were the ages at which the parents first typically allowed their children to spend unsupervised time after school on a regular basis. In their national survey, Hofferth, Brayfield, Deich, and Holcomb (1991) also found that the percentage of children in self-care rose dramatically in these years. Whereas only 11% of children ages 8 to 10 regularly cared for themselves at some point during a typical week, 40% of the 12-year-olds did so.

Although some children in our study spent only a few hours a week without adult supervision, others were unsupervised for more lengthy periods. Several parents either had professional jobs that required frequent work away from home on evenings and weekends, or held multiple jobs or jobs with evening shifts. Twelve-year-old Layla Williams, whose single-parent mother sometimes worked as many as 100 hours a week, rarely saw her parent during waking hours. Although Layla spent some of her after-school hours in a local drop-in program, she spent most of her evening time with her 14-year-old brother or alone.

Children often became unsupervised because situational constraints made adult supervision difficult or impossible. In many cases, children lost their eligibility for after-school programs when they reached a certain age, and no reliable substitute could be found. (In the communities where the research was conducted, as in most communities nationwide, virtually no formal after-school programs extended beyond the fourth or fifth grade.) Sometimes an adult who supervised the child in earlier years moved out of the household. One family moved to a community that lacked an appropriate after-school program, and another child's program closed because of financial problems. Parents in some cases could not afford after-school care for their children or found the cost of after-school supervision unacceptably high. Sometimes, after-school programs that were appealing in themselves were made unattractive by the logistics involved in attending them. Several families were deterred from otherwise desirable programs by the long walk that children would have returning home. The walk might be considered too fatiguing at the end of a long day, or it might be considered dangerous, particularly after dark and in high crime neighborhoods.

Many parents who successfully arrange supervision for their children on regular school days are unable to do so when there are school holidays or early release days, or when their children are ill. In one year, Irene Castillo's after-school program closed six times for bad weather and also on occasions when both the after-school teachers were ill. Children often first experience unsupervised time during such breaks from the normal routine. If this initiation into unsupervised time is reasonably successful, parents and children may become more comfortable with the idea of unsupervised time and may choose it for regular afternoons.

Parents also talk with their friends and the parents of their children's friends and influence each other's thinking about after-school arrangements. When some children make the move to unsupervised time, other children may soon follow. Before she allowed Diana to come home unsupervised, Tricia Hardy noted that some of Diana's friends were beginning to be allowed to come home after school without adult supervision. That "seemed like not such a bad idea. Most kids seemed to really not like the after-school program." Soon Diana was allowed to come home on her own, too. Emilie Perry says that it was her own friends who convinced her to allow Jasmin to be unsupervised after school. "Basically, my friends who have kids the same age talked me into it." Meiguei Chen's mother reassures herself that her daughter is better off in the library after school, rather than in an after-school program, "because I hear my friend's kids complain. Of the two, I think the library is better."

Although parents often report an increase in worry when their children stop attending after-school programs and begin spending unsupervised time at home after school, they also often report that their own lives are simplified. Instead of hurrying to pick up their children at the after-school program by a certain time they are able to head directly home after work. Children can take messages for their parents, do a bit of housework, or even start the family dinner. Saving the cost of after-school care is also a significant benefit for many families.

Changes in family composition can also precipitate the move to self-care. Until his parents divorced, Carl Peters and his older brother were supervised after school by their father, who was unemployed. After the divorce, Suzanne Peters hired babysitters, but the boys resented this and pushed for more independence. Suzanne allowed them to come home on their own when Carl was 9 and Seth was 12, although their still-unemployed father lived nearby and presumably would have continued to supervise the boys if the marriage had not ended.

Eric Holden's sequence of after-school arrangements reflects the many changes in his family life over the years. In first grade he attended an after-school program in Wisconsin; then, when his family moved to the Boston area, he was supervised after school by his mother's unemployed friend. In second grade, Eric went to live with his uncle and aunt in Minnesota. During that time, one of the adults, who worked different shifts, was always home when he returned from school. Eric moved back to his mother's household in third grade, and at first went home after school to be cared for by his mother's roommate. When the friend moved out, Eric's mother was unable to find a place for him at the local after-school program, so he began going home after school, staying inside the house by himself until his mother returned from work.

Although contextual factors seem to have been powerful in moving many children into self-care, children themselves often precipitated the change, preferring the independence of self-care to what were perceived as "babyish" or unappealing after-school programs. When Nate Kelley was in fourth grade and his sister, Michelle, in third, neither wanted to attend an after-school program, which they saw as being "for little kids." Several children were described as "day-cared out" or "burnt out" on formal after-school programs. Other children needed more time for homework than their after-school programs allowed, or wanted to pursue specialized lessons or activities that were incompatible with attendance at a regular after-school program. Some children wanted time to "veg out" after the demands of the school day. J. Steinberg and Riley (n.d.) discussed such concerns as representing "developmental press for self care":

> Developmental press, as we use the term, refers to normal processes of development that lead a child to push against existing environmental constraints, and/or to seek out new environments in which to exercise newly emerging capacities. For example, a child developing the capacity for autonomous, self-responsible behavior may, after six or seven hours of adult-directed school activity, rebel against adults who structure after-school programs too tightly, or may lobby parents for an expansion of self-responsibility in the after-school hours. (pp. 5–6)

When Stacey Moore began working full time again after years of part-time work, her 10- and 12-year-old daughters refused to go to after-school programs. "Barbara felt and Bonita agreed that having been in programs since they were little, that they were tired of a structured program that they had to follow." And, as Mark (their father) pointed out, they were used to coming home. Instead of attending an after-school program, they proposed developing their own schedule of activities within the neighborhood. There was an elderly neighbor nearby who knew them and could help out in an emergency, and both parents worked only blocks away from the house. The girls have been on their own after school ever since.

After-school programs often seem to serve the needs of younger children better than the needs of older ones, and many children move out of these programs as they become less appealing over time. Diana Hardy had been in after-school programs since kindergarten and these were fine, according to her mother, "especially when Diana was younger. They did lots of arts and crafts and took kids out to play." Then the program became more expensive, and Tricia Hardy moved Diana to a different, more affordable after-school program. This program proved far less appealing. "When I went to pick her up they'd have all the kids in one big room. Five minutes of it would be awful even for me. It was awful overstimulation." Tricia remembered how she felt after a day at school and how nice it was to be able to come home. She decided to allow Diana to leave the program and come home, too.

Tricia does not regret the decision. She thinks the best things for Diana about her unsupervised arrangement are

> being able to come home. Being able to have unstructured time. Being able to relax after school. Having flexibility. Being able to decide last minute that she wants to play with another friend. . . . In after-school you have to be with a group of kids and have to get along, have to socialize. At home there's more pressure to be resourceful, which I suppose is positive.

However, Tricia does not like Diana spending so much time alone or feeling that if Diana needs something there may not be somebody to give it to her.

> I'd like to be able to be here to help her get better organized when she gets home and also to have somebody she can talk to and spew out to after the day at school. . . . I think she wishes I were here every day when she got home. Aside from that, I know she prefers it to an after-school program.

Tricia also pays a price with her own anxiety about Diana's unsupervised time.

> It puts more pressure on me worrying about what she's doing in the afternoon. From 3 p.m. on I can't be totally relaxed. I'm thinking about whether she's home, doing homework.

When Justin Stiles was younger, his aunt watched him during the after-school hours. When she moved out of state, Justin began attending the after-school program at his school. As his mother, Rhonda, said, "Since there was a program in the school it seemed appropriate for me to have him with the teachers who were trained to work with kids." Justin is now 9 years old, and both his parents are very pleased with the after-school program. Leonard Stiles believes Justin is exposed to good things and learns a lot, and that the teachers at the after-school program treat him well and seem very concerned. In addition, "it makes me feel more secure knowing that he's got someone looking after him." He also believes that Justin loves the program, although he is not sure which activities he likes best. "I never really got into detail on that with him, to be honest." It is impressive to Leonard that his son chooses to spend time at the program. "Yesterday he came home and my wife was home, and he said, 'I want to go back to the after-school.' So we told him, 'go ahead' [laughs]." Leonard doesn't think there is anything his son would rather be doing after school. "No, not really, because what else could he do? Get into trouble? Watch television? No. I think he's very comfortable there."

For Rhonda, the best things about Justin's after-school program is that it

> relieves me of the fear of him being caught on the streets unattended. He's playing with a selected group of kids. He's not trapped to the TV. I feel comfortable with the program and the teachers. We have open conferences. We can discuss the kids' behavior after a stressful day at school. He likes the field trips. He likes meeting other kids from other schools and sharing the experiences [not just the same kids he sees all day long].

Justin's favorite activity, according to Rhonda, is playing basketball. Like her husband, Rhonda says there is really nothing she does not like about the program. "I have no qualms about it because I like the teachers and feel comfortable with them."

However, Rhonda believes that Justin is not so content. "He's getting to the point where he thinks he's too big for after-school care because he's the oldest in his group. He has his good days because he has challenges but he feels he's too good." Rhonda believes "he'd rather be with older kids, not so much out of after-school but in a program with older kids." She worries about what will happen when he grows out of the program, which only lasts until fourth grade.

> He's still young, so I'll have to find someone in the neighborhood or leave him unattended. In a program he doesn't feel like he's a little kid being with a babysitter. He has other kids with him. I don't worry that he's not coming straight home, or is playing with the stove or something. It's very scary to leave them unattended. There is a feeling of security with the program.

Justin reflects the discontent about the program to which his mother alluded. He likes the program best "when you get to go to the gym and when you get to go on field trips." As his mother thought, his favorite activity is playing basketball. But he does not like it "when there is nothing to do." He says he dislikes his after-school arrangements somewhat and thinks some of his friends have more fun than he does after school. "They get to do things that I don't get to do, like go to the store, and I have to stay at the afterschool." Justin would prefer staying home alone. "I would watch TV and do my homework." His favorite time of day is "when I get to stay home and watch TV."

In the second year of our study, Justin does leave his after-school program, which only accepts younger children, and begins coming home on his own. According to Rhonda, "Sometimes his dad is here, but 90% of the time he's by himself."

She believes that being on his own gives Justin "a sense of independence" and makes him responsible. It "helps him get over his fear of being alone." Rhonda has asked Justin how he feels about coming home alone, and he has told her it is not a problem for him. "He likes it this way. It's quiet and relaxing. He can unwind from the day." Rhonda believes that what Justin likes best about the arrangement is coming home and watching television. "He doesn't do his homework, so that's not it. It probably relaxes him from the stress of the day. Sometimes he falls asleep." An additional benefit of the arrangement is a financial one. "I save his after-school tuition money. That's the only gain because he does get bored." Rhonda calls Justin from work to see how his day was and to break the monotony for her son, "because I know he's coming home to an empty house," and she believes the calls help him feel secure.

Rhonda has many worries, however, about the arrangement:

> It exposes him to much older kids who are in the wrong clique. I can only believe he's here when he says he is because I can't keep calling. It's leaving him exposed. Being alone, even for an adult, is freaky. It gets too quiet.

She also worries about Justin preparing food. "He likes to cook and I worry about safety." Rhonda says that Justin is not allowed to go to the town center and hang out in stores. "He has older friends who do that [hang out] even though they don't have money." Justin has one older friend he is very close to, and he is allowed to go to the friend's house. The friend is not allowed to visit Justin, however. Rhonda fears that once in the house, the friend will manipulate Justin, getting him into trouble because it is not his own home that is at risk. At another point in the interview, Rhonda says that Justin "doesn't get into trouble, not yet anyway."

UNACKNOWLEDGED LACK OF SUPERVISION

Children sometimes appear to slip into unsupervised arrangements without the active awareness of their parents. For several years, Mary Ellen Kelliher spent much of her after-school time with a close family friend, a licensed day-care provider who lived a few doors away from the Kelliher family. According to Darlene Kelliher, this arrangement continued until Mary Ellen was 11 years old. Yet when Mary Ellen was 10 years old, she no longer mentioned going to the neighbor's house in the afternoons, and told the interviewer that she went home to play, watch television, and do homework after school. Perhaps the disagreement is partially a semantic one, because supervision can be an elastic concept. Darlene may consider Mary Ellen supervised if the family friend is available to her in the afternoons, whereas Mary Ellen may prefer to think of herself as unsupervised.

Although in the Kelliher family it seems that the child is slipping away from adult supervision, in the Berger family it appears that the parent is elusive. Carol Berger tells the interviewer that she is usually home when her daughter, Marguerite, returns from school each day, and this is reasonable because Carol works as an assistant teacher and completes work at about the same time Marguerite finishes school. Marguerite tells her interviewer, however, that her mother is home in the afternoon only "occasionally," and that she really does not know where her mother is after school. If she needed to reach her she would call her mother's friend to find out where she is.

These discrepancies between the reports of family members are reminiscent of the low rates of agreement Richardson et al. (1989) found when they compared parent and child reports of the extent of unsupervised after-school time. What is particularly striking in this study is that these discrepant pictures of after-school supervision were given by parents and children interviewed simultaneously and in adjacent rooms.

When understandings of children's after-school time use differed sharply between family members, it often seemed that these parents and children were able to satisfy their own wishes about the child's after-school time. Perhaps their discrepant understandings actually reduced tensions between family members by providing each a more satisfying image of reality.

CHANGES IN UNSUPERVISED ARRANGEMENTS OVER TIME

When children first become unsupervised, parents generally make great efforts to stay in close touch with them and often promulgate many rules to govern the use of after-school time. As time goes on, however, these efforts often diminish as parents feel greater confidence in their children's abilities to handle unsupervised time and children feel greater comfort in their situations. Reflecting back on her earlier behavior, Stacey Moore remembers that when her daughters were younger she called them every day. "It's no longer an issue. And before I worked only a few blocks away and now I work downtown. You'd think I'd be more anxious, but I'm not." Her daughter does not "check in" with her now, as she was required to do in the past. Stacey sees this change as "a developmental thing." Micah Somers' mother says that the rules governing the after-school hours "change all the time. As the kids get older they are no longer applicable. Situations change. New issues come up. New needs."

RESPONSIBILITIES

For several children in the study, the move to self-care is part of a larger move toward taking responsibility for the running of the household. In some cases, children supervise younger siblings, do substantial housework, and prepare the family's evening meal during their after-school hours.

Four days a week, Ruby Nelson, a single parent, does not get home from her job until 7 p.m. Her 12-year-old daughter, Dominique takes responsibility for her own schoolwork, the housework, and for 5-year-old sister Linnell without waiting for her mother to direct her. Dominique made up her own rule about homework: She does it right after school, when she gets home. She started doing this on her own and it became a habit. According to Ruby, Dominique has no rules about chores either. On a typical afternoon she might do the laundry, the dishes, and clean her room. Ruby says, "She is good about doing things around the house on her own."

In the Townsend family, 10-year-old George spends after-school time with 6-year-old Michael. The boys are home by 2:30 p.m., and they clean their rooms, do homework, and then go out to play, where they stay within "eye's reach" of each other. Eleanor Townsend's brother lives with the family and checks in with the boys occasionally, when his work schedule allows. When the boys are outside, George is in charge, although Eleanor emphasizes that they are both responsible for following her instructions. She returns home from work about 5:30 p.m.

In this study, children in low-income families and in single-parent households were particularly likely to become sibling caretakers. Among children with siblings, almost three-fourths of those from single-parent, low-income families cared for their siblings after school, whereas fewer than one quarter of those from moderate or high-income, two-parent families did so. Such findings are in line with previous research suggesting that children's responsibilities are greater in single-parent than in two-parent households (Weiss, 1979) and with the general principle offered by Whiting and Whiting (1975), that the degree to which children are expected to be responsible and independent from adults is predicted by the extent of women's work loads. In the present study, African-American children were also particularly likely to be sibling caretakers, which is hardly surprising because these children were also overrepresented in low-income and single-parent households. Cutler et al. (1995) similarly found sibling caretaking to be particularly prevalent in African-American households. In their study, self-care was used almost twice as frequently by Whites and Hispanic families as by African-American families, whereas sibling care was used far more frequently by African Americans than by Whites or Hispanics. In Cutler et al.'s study, ethnicity was even more important than parents' marital status in predicting the use of sibling care.

BECOMING SUPERVISED AGAIN

Although most children moved from supervised to unsupervised settings over the course of the study, several children moved against the current, from unsupervised to supervised settings. Children who moved from unsupervised to supervised conditions generally did so because of a change in family circumstance, such as a mother spending time at home on maternity leave, a parent losing a job, or an adult relative moving into the house. When children became supervised for such reasons, there was often little impact on the previously unsupervised child.

Stacey Moore left her job and was looking for a new one at the time of our second set of interviews with the family, but she said that her own lack of employment really did not affect her daughters' largely unsupervised after-school time. Eleven-year-old Bonita and 13-year-old Barbara are so busy with their activities in and out of the house, that they spend very little time with their mother when she is at home after school. "I feel like an intruder sometimes. It's kind of funny. I don't see much of them at all." Jane Kelley, whose children have been on their own for several years, says that "even when I am here, it is as if I don't exist." She feels less pressure to rush out of work as early as possible or to take work home with her than she felt when her children were first unsupervised after school. Timothy Kelley also works at home during the final year of the study, and his 14-year-old son is not particularly appreciative. Nate says, "When my dad was away the whole day, I liked it. I had the house to myself. Now he's home more and that's okay, but it was better before."

Sometimes, however, children were provided greater adult supervision in response to a specific problem or crisis. Nick Lavelle took care of his younger sister, Violet, until she began to have epileptic seizures. Then his mother put Violet into an after-school program "because it was too much to ask of him and she needed adult supervision." Between the time we recruited his family for the study and our first interviews with them, 12-year-old Eric Holden was caught cutting school and stealing from cars. His mother responded by bringing Eric to work with her after school and on most school vacation days. Her boss was "really marvelous," truly supportive of Eric's being there. However, this arrangement was seen as temporary. After several weeks, Eric returned to spending afternoons unsupervised at home. During the remainder of the study, Eric never again got into such dramatic trouble, but his mother worried that he was still not mature enough to spend so much of his time unsupervised and alone.

When she was 11, Patricia MacCarthy attended orchestra rehearsals after school and did some babysitting, but she spent most of her after-school time home alone with her older sister doing chores and homework. Patricia could only leave the house or have friends over if she had completed her homework and finished her chores and was not being punished for earlier lapses, and apparently this rarely happened. (During an interview in February she told the interviewer she had been "grounded" since the beginning of the school year.) Patricia also reported little support and much "bossing" from her older sister, Karen. Between the second and third set of interviews, severe problems became evident in the MacCarthy family. Karen ran away from home and moved in with their aunt. Patricia also ran away, was raped, and then tried to kill herself. As a consequence of these events, the state Department of Social Services intervened in the family and arranged a variety of activities and therapeutic services for Patricia on weekday afternoons.

When we first interviewed her, Cynthia Edwards had a semi-supervised arrangement in the afternoons after school. Her mother, Terry, was home with her but was generally asleep, because she worked the midnight shift. This meant that Cynthia could not disturb her unless there was an emergency. When we went back the following year, Terry was still working nights and sleeping days, but Cynthia was busy three afternoons a week with after-school activities: movies, gymnastics, and a cooking class. Her mother explained that this was now possible because she had "relaxed a little bit and asked her daddy for some help." The extra money allowed Terry to provide interesting activities and real human companionship to her daughter during the after-school hours, resolving some of the problems the first-year interview had highlighted. In the final year of the study, Terry quit the night shift and was able to be with her daughter in the late afternoons and all night long. These changes over the course of the study toward greater supervision and companionship pleased Cynthia very much. And each of these changes cost money, either to pay for after-school activities or to forego the higher income that comes with nighttime work.

The present study converges with cross-sectional studies in finding that older children are more likely than younger children to experience self-care, but the longitudinal nature of the present study also reveals that children sometimes move "backwards" from self-care or sibling care to adult supervision. When previously unsupervised children return to adult supervision almost accidentally, because parents are between jobs or an adult relative moves into the household, the supervision seems less rigorous than is typical for children who have never been in self-care. In contrast, adult supervision may be especially intense when children reenter supervision in response to a personal or family crisis.

Over the 4 years of this study almost all of the children spent some unsupervised time after school, although self-care came earlier for some children than for others. It may be more useful to ask when the children of employed parents become unsupervised rather than whether they do so. The near universality of self-care should not be surprising because few communities have after-school programs that serve children beyond Grades 4 or 5. With grandparents and other relatives likely to be employed themselves and acceptable paid babysitters difficult to find, self-care becomes the only remaining option for many families with employed parents. In hard-pressed single-parent and low-income families, children are often needed as caretakers for their younger siblings.

Yet these situational factors do not explain all of the movement away from supervised after-school time over the course of the study. Dissatisfaction with existing programs and a wish for more freedom in the after-school hours prompt many children to lobby their parents for unsupervised arrangements. More strikingly, many parents are convinced by their children's arguments. Those concerned with school-aged child care must take seriously the views of those parents and children who are not satisfied with the after-school programs they have experienced or who find these programs less attractive than unsupervised arrangements.

6

Stressful Challenges in the After-School Hours

Zack Monroe was 11 years old, in sixth grade, and participating in a selective program for academically talented students when we first interviewed him. The only child of a single mother, Zack has very little contact with his father. Because of the extra homework he is required to do for his academic program, Zack no longer goes after school to the community center he attended when he was younger. Instead, his mother allows him to spend time on his own so that he can go to the library and concentrate on his schoolwork.

Zack's mother, Peggy, describes Zack's after-school arrangement as "more like no arrangement at all." After school Zack is supposed to do his homework in the library, go home, or go to a friend's house. However, Zack rarely gets his homework done. "Most kids go to the library and get their homework done, but I go there and fool around." Zack's inability to complete his homework, despite the intelligence and skills that brought him to his accelerated program, have put him in danger of failing his classes.

Peggy has a professional job that often requires her to work evenings, and on these days "Zack has to be totally responsible for himself. It extends beyond after-school care. He's responsible for feeding himself, doing his homework, and taking his bath." Zack and Peggy both describe Zack as a fine cook, but he apparently has difficulty preparing meals when he is on his own. Even when Peggy fixes dinner for Zack and leaves it ready for him, he often does not eat when she is not with him. Peggy frequently arrives home on such evenings to discover that Zack has eaten nothing, has left his homework undone, and has failed to straighten up the apartment as he was asked to do. Zack had health problems during the study period, and Peggy believes they are exacerbated when Zack doesn't eat. On days when Zack is sick or on days when school is closed, Zack stays home alone. Peggy says, "When he's sick I know he'd like more attention. All kids need their mothers when they're sick and he's been sick a lot this year."

Peggy is extremely important to Zack, and he often misses her when she is not with him. He understands that as an only parent, "you have to work," but "sometimes I really want to be with my mother when she's working." He does visit Peggy at work about two or three times a week, even though Peggy finds these visits disruptive. He wishes he could have more time "just to talk with her, but she never seems to have free time." Interview questions on loneliness often evoke thoughts of his mother. He has a tough time responding to a question concerning how often he feels lonely, commenting that he is lonely "when I'm not with my mom and I want to be with her and talk with her. I'm not lonely when I'm with friends." When asked what he would do if he were home alone and became lonely or bored, he responds, "That's usually when I want to be with my mom." Things that make Zack feel worried or sad include bad grades and "my mother being disappointed in me."

Peggy would like to hire someone to be at the apartment when Zack returns from school, but lack of money is an obstacle. She considers Zack's after-school arrangements a very emotional issue:

> I feel really bad. He is too young to be left alone so much. And I feel guilty when he's sick or when he is fearful. Sometimes when I come home at night after having worked late, he'll have an old golf club out for protection. Yet he doesn't mention it to me. And I also worry because this is a big burglary neighborhood. [Their apartment actually was robbed during the

> course of the study when neither Zack nor Peggy were at home.] What if he is home alone and someone tries to break in?

Although Peggy sees the dangers to Zack of being on his own, her earlier efforts to provide him protection and supervision once had tragic consequences for which she also blames herself. When Zack was 7 years old he was sexually abused in their apartment by a babysitter who had been recommended to Peggy by the staff at Zack's after-school program. "If I had been home, not working, it wouldn't have happened. Or if I had taken the time to screen this babysitter or scout out other sitters, it wouldn't have happened. Zack did tell me, but it had been going on for some time. We've both been in therapy as a result of it."

After-school arrangements present a variety of challenges to children. Many of these challenges are more frequent among children who are without adult supervision. Yet challenge and stress are not limited to children in unsupervised settings.

DANGER

Stephanie Samuels worries about what would happen in a true emergency when her daughter, Julie, is home alone.

> As adults we can have plans and still, unanticipated things come up. Will my little kid carry out the plan, and remember that her safety is the most important thing? . . . I don't mean to imply that I worry about it all the time. I review things with her, but I don't want to overdo it and get her filled with fear.

Emma Lavelle says, "I try to fight in myself real fears from others—you know—the milk carton thing. I don't really think they'll be kidnapped but I fight that fear." Stacey Moore says she does not worry about her daughters getting into mischief, "because I've taught them and they're responsible. . . . It's the unknown, someone following them home, not their behavior." When Adam Stone is on his own, his mother is comforted by her religious faith. "I'm religious. I believe God is with him." Emilie Perry's daughter is on her own a good deal, too, and, she says, "I'd blame myself if anything happened to her."

Several of the children in the study did encounter frightening emergencies while they were at home alone or with siblings. Although none of these emergencies led to crippling injuries, they were highly upsetting when they happened. Jasmin Perry stepped on a nail and could not remove it from her foot. Christopher Jones cut himself with a sharp knife. Carl Peters fell and broke his arm while playing basketball. Tanisha Wright, at 7 years of age, somehow got into the family car, moving it out of the driveway and into the street. Fortunately, a neighbor was able to remove the nail from Jasmin's foot. Christopher's older brother, Omar, called the ambulance, the police, then his grandparents and parents. Carl was taken to the hospital in an ambulance by his older brother when their mother could not be reached. Tanisha was not hurt, and her older brother, Jeffrey, was able to calm her down and find neighbors who helped return the car to the driveway.

FEAR

Whether or not they experience objective dangers, children often experience fears when they are on their own. Strange noises, disturbing telephone calls, or just the silence of an empty house may trigger anxiety. In some cases, an adult might view the child's fears as unrealistic. In other cases, children seem less afraid than adults believe they should be.

Diana Hardy, age 10, says it sometimes gets a little scary when she is home on her own: "I think someone's watching. One time someone was but it was a boy, not a man. So it wasn't as scary as if an adult was watching me 'cause a boy couldn't do as much harm." The day before our first interview with Diana she received a series of suspicious telephone calls. "I went to call the police and as I was calling Mom came home and scared me half to death." Diana reassures herself in several ways. "One good thing is that I carry a heavy bookbag so if anyone tries to get me I can go 'whack'[hit them with the bookbag]." Television and her kitten help calm her after a fright. Diana believes that she is getting better at aspects of being by herself

> like answering the door and telephone and weird calls and stuff and feeling I'm being followed. I usually panicked and stayed in one place and wouldn't move. I wouldn't move a muscle and would try not to breathe so

> if someone came in they'd think I was dead. But then they could take my pulse.

Julie Samuels never feels scared or uncomfortable when she is with her friends after school, although no adults are present, but she has felt this way a few times when she was home alone. "Sometimes I get these crazy daydreams someone is going to come in, kidnap me, and kill me and when my mom passes the cemetery she'll see my name on a gravestone." Julie says she only felt a little scared, and the feeling "just kind of went away," so she did not mention it to her mother. "I didn't think it was that important. It was just a daydream. It probably wasn't going to happen. Only about a 1% chance it would happen."

Eight-year-old Cynthia Edwards says she believes in monsters and thinks they are hiding in her closet. Her single-parent mother works the night shift and her older brother is often away from home. Cynthia sometimes has problems sleeping at night because she is frightened in her empty apartment and thinks she hears keys at the door, someone trying to break in. She has told her mother about hearing noises at the doors, but "she thinks I'm making it up." According to Terry Edwards, Cynthia recently left the door open an inch or two "and I pointed out to her anybody trying to get in wouldn't need keys." Terry believes that Cynthia does not have this fear on the nights that she (Terry) is home.

Twelve-year-old Carl Peters and his mother have very different notions of what constitutes a dangerous situation. Suzanne Peters believes that Carl is sometimes scared when he is home alone, more so at night, but also in the afternoon. She says that when he is home alone, he gets out a knife. She believes that his fear is irrational, a phobia, because he recently wanted to walk to a dangerous part of town at 11 p.m. to rent a movie. Because he did not show any concern for his safety in what was to her a clearly dangerous situation, it is irrational that he should show so much concern in a situation she believes is much less threatening.

In his interview, however, Carl claims his house has been broken into twice while he was home alone. Once he says he came on an intruder upstairs in the house and the man left by the back door. The other time he came home and found the door ajar. He claims he was only scared the first time, and then he felt a little nervous for a couple of weeks when he was home by himself. Suzanne Peters also describes an incident in which Carl played a "prank" on his older brother, Seth, that involved messing up the house while Seth was out to make it look like it had been broken into. Seth called the police, and Carl later admitted to staging the incident. Suzanne believes that Carl was acting out his worst fears.

SELF-REGULATION

As Zack Monroe expresses it, "I'm having a serious problem with discipline." According to Zack, on a typical day, "I come home and I'm having some trouble doing homework recently, and I read, mostly for pleasure, until Mom comes home. Then I pretend I'm doing homework. I used to watch TV, but it got a little addictive so I put that away for awhile."

Peggy Monroe says that Zack is months behind in his homework, and that she has had to go to several meetings with his teachers to discuss this problem. About the only way Zack will do any homework is with his mother sitting right beside him. He has told Peggy that his former scout master sat with his son when he was having problems completing homework. Peggy seems quite angry about this because she works very long hours and does not want to come home and have to argue with Zack or sit with him while he does his homework. She feels homework is his responsibility, and he should have it done by the time she gets home.

One of the most crucial challenges to children in the after-school hours is moment-to-moment self-regulation (Maccoby, 1984). Children need to comply with appropriate rules and guidelines for behavior, avoid undue risks, and complete required tasks, often without adult assistance or prodding. This proves a particularly difficult challenge for some.

Parents generally provide rules to guide their children during unsupervised time. In some cases, these rules are followed with complete success. In other cases, the rules are bent or broken when parents are not around to monitor children.

Eleven-year-old Layla Williams' single-parent mother, Jocelyn, works two and sometimes three jobs to provide the family with an approximation of a middle-class lifestyle, and Layla and her brother rarely see their mother during the week. Jocelyn may be physically absent, but her rules govern and organize the time her children spend without her. As she says, "I know how to run my home, even when I'm not there." The children must call her when they get home from school. They must do their homework, with the television off, before they can go outside to play. If they have no homework, they must spend some time studying. Jocelyn checks their homework when she comes home from work, and if it is not correct and neat, they must do it over. After they do their homework, they are allowed to go out and play right outside their building until dark. They must call Jocelyn before they leave the building and again when they return. They can have approved friends over if they behave properly. When Layla and Andrew come inside for the evening they prepare their own dinners and then wash the dishes. After that they do their chores, which include such things as cleaning their rooms, doing laundry, and vacuuming. They are then free to do what they want to do until Jocelyn comes home. If they fail to do what they are supposed to, they are not allowed to go outside to play the next day. Although Layla is the younger child, Jocelyn does not regard Andrew as her caretaker. Although the children should look out for each other, they are primarily responsible for themselves.

Jocelyn finds it reassuring to know that when she works she does not have to worry about her children. She describes how she started teaching her children to act responsibly when they were young, first explaining to them why she had to work such long hours.

> Discipline is the key. Other parents complain to me about their kids, but I believe it is a lack of training. I keep on the kids. It's how you raise your child. Other people can't even work one job without getting calls at work, people telling them their kids are having problems. If you were raised with working parents, you know what it is like, what it requires. I never have anyone complain to me about my kids.

Layla describes her after-school time and the rules that govern it in the same way her mother does. As she says, "I know what are the things that need to be done, so I do it." She also chooses afternoon as her favorite time of day. "cause I get to play outside and do more things." Things that make her feel happy include "'cleaning up my room," as well as watching television and playing with other children.

Stacey Moore describes her girls as having already internalized the rules that govern their after-school time. About homework she says, "It's just expected that it's done—unvoiced expectations." About having friends over she says, "No rules if it's friends we know, but they usually ask." The girls can cook as long as they clean up afterward, and sometimes they make dinner for the family. The girls have to monitor their own television viewing. "Barbara spends much more time reading. Bonita has to monitor herself and tells me she'll cut back [on television]. Her conscience bothers her because she knows we don't like it."

Terry Edwards says that her daughter would answer the door when she is home alone "whether I said to or not." Terry hesitates to talk with Cynthia about the "sick people out there," like rapists and muggers, "because I don't know the line between informing and frightening." According to Terry, Cynthia already worries about enough things without having to worry about everyone on the street.

Zack Monroe and his mother, Peggy, describe Zack's rules and responsibilities for after-school time in somewhat discrepant ways. Peggy says that she does not like Zack to have friends over when he is on his own. Zack thinks it is all right to have friends over as long as they "don't stay for hours." Peggy says that Zack is supposed to clean his room and take out the garbage. Zack thinks he has no chores. Most importantly, Peggy says that Zack is supposed to have completed all his homework before Peggy comes home. Zack believes there are no "real" family rules about homework. Zack seems to know what his mother would like him to do, but he does not always abide by her wishes. He reports that he recently went to the video arcade after school, but said, "Don't tell my mother." In a later year of the study Zack says, "there really are no rules." Peggy's perspective is that Zack's rules change "because they are not being observed. I just yield."

Eric Holden's single-parent mother has a full-time job and also goes to school two evenings a week, arriving home on these days at 8:30 or 9 p.m. Before his mother comes home, 13-year-old Eric is supposed to wash the dishes, pick up the living room, make his mother's bed (he earns money for this), and take out the trash. On the evenings his mother is in school, Eric is also responsible for making dinner. He is encouraged to do his homework after school, although he does not need to finish it before his mother comes home. What Eric likes least about his after-school time is

> when I talk on the phone all afternoon and then Mom calls and says she's coming home. I have to get all the chores done. I feel bad, upset, if Mom calls me and I didn't do the chores. Mom doesn't want me talking so much. But if I didn't get to talk to friends, I'd be upset.

Eric says that he often fails to follow his after-school rules, and that his mother generally figures this out.

> She can tell if I don't have homework done or I'm gone too long. Sometimes she knows if a friend is over. She finds evidence, like shoe prints on the floor. She'll look in my room and see the chairs were moved. She'll say, "You had a friend over." I'll say, "No." Then she'll say, "Why were the chairs moved?"

Eric's mother is also troubled that he lets into the apartment people he does not know, which is in violation of her explicit rule.

> It's hard for kids. You don't want to make them paranoid, but they should be realistically cautious. That is something that makes me really nervous. He'll let people in sometimes. That's the worst part of him staying home [alone] after school.

Jessica Holden needs Eric's help with household work because her own workload is so heavy, yet she is aware hat these chores are a burden to her son. She does not feel she can really trust Eric's friends in the apartment, yet she believes that Eric is terribly lonely in the afternoons, and that this loneliness is also making him angry, sad, reserved, and perhaps depressed. Her eyes fill with tears as she describes her frustration. In consultation with Eric's psychologist, she later relieves Eric of his cooking responsibilities and allows him to have friends over.

In the Kelley family, parents and children are aware that unsupervised time after school allows the children to bend or break household rules. Yet, significantly, only some rules are broken, and these rules do not concern safety. When asked what she likes best about being home on her own, Michelle says, "I get to do things I'm not allowed to do, like eat junk food and do homework in front of the TV." She is only allowed to watch 1 hour of television a day, but when she is alone she says she watches more. Her brother, Nate, reports the same television rule—"Mom says not more than one hour," but also reports additional television viewing. Jane Kelley, however, is not in the dark. When asked whether the children follow the house rule forbidding television while doing homework, she says, "I think it is a safe bet to say they sneak it." Perhaps breaking rules is something of a family theme. Nate reports that when he went to visit his father at work, he discovered him "cheating," that is, still smoking cigarettes after promising to stop.

Yet bending or breaking rules ends when safety is involved. Timothy Kelley explains that Michelle and her brother have rules about answering the door when they are home alone. They can see who is at the door, and they are not supposed to let anyone in unless they know them. Timothy proudly reports that one day the cable television installer came and Michelle would not let him in. The workman said to her, "Well, it's now or never," and she replied, "Well, then, I guess it's never."

In the Kelley family, the rules governing unsupervised time also change as the years go by. In the third year of the study Timothy says:

> In a sense, I would say we really don't have rules for the kids anymore. They know what the expectations are—we don't have to say it. The rules are only implied, not explicit. The kids have internalized well what to do. We're more interested in their learning how to handle various situations as they come up. We want them to be responsible enough to figure out what to do. . . . Nate, now that he is a seventh grader, is really into pushing things to their limits. He has been coming up with any number of reasons to infringe on the rules. He's learned how to circumvent the rules. He's managed to show us he understands the difference between the letter and the spirit of the law. We let him get away with breaking the rules if he can give us a reasonable defense of his actions. We do this because of the value we have always placed on reason.

In the Kelley family, the demands for self-regulation increase over time, as the children demonstrate their ability to behave safely and properly when they are away from adults, and their parents remove some of the scaffolding that has regulated the children's behavior.

STRUCTURE

After-school settings differ in the extent to which they structure children's use of time. Activities such as supervised team sports, music lessons, and dance lessons provide adult-initiated structure. After-school programs often allow children to choose among a variety of structured activities and sometimes allow children the option of time that is not directly organized by adults. Adults who supervise children in their own homes may or may not suggest or organize things for the children to do. When children are unsupervised, parental rules, and guidelines (*distal supervision*) may help to provide structure. Occasionally, other children may offer a child a structured activity. Neighborhood children in the park may have begun a pick-up game of softball that other children may join. Yet it is often up to the child herself to create an appealing structure to the afternoon.

Children who spend their after-school time in chosen structured activities are generally pleased with what they do, but sometimes wish for more free, unstructured time. Micah Somers and his older sister fill much of their after-school time with an array of sports programs, music lessons, and dance classes. "They lead very busy lives," as their mother says. She believes that they enjoy it "because they choose the activities." But she also believes "they would prefer a less hectic schedule and more unstructured time just to play with their friends or with their toys." According to Peter Somers, Micah especially likes the unstructured free time he does have. "The value of it is really felt," because Micah can compare it with the structured time he spends. "I think you could pick any one day and he'd say he'd rather be playing with his friends in the park. But that would wear thin. It's like someone wanting dessert every day."

Micah says that he enjoys what he does after school, but comments that he is often so busy, there is "no time to stop and say, 'hmm.'" What would be good, according to Micah, "would be if there were more days in the week, and then I could play with my friends more." Partly in response to such concerns, the family each year takes a 2-month summer vacation by the sea. This period of unstructured time complements their demanding schedules during the school year.

Some children in the study were capable of structuring their own time, without adult supervision or even much guidance from adults. Barbara and Bonita Moore convinced their parents they were ready to spend time on their own when their mother, Stacey, went back to work full time one summer. Stacey insisted that the girls could not be home alone all day, "so they came up with a longer, more complicated schedule that they preferred to day camp. . . . The only difference between it and a scheduled day camp was that it was their schedule." The girls staged their own Olympics (both girls are serious athletes), a fair (for which they did their own baking), picnics, trips to the local park, and swimming at a nearby pool. They also wrote, produced, and performed their own play, making their own costumes.

Jasmin Perry is largely unsupervised during the week, but she has imposed a kind of structure on her after-school time. On Monday she comes home and starts her homework by 2:30. Then she calls her friend, Lena, and goes out with her afterward. On Tuesday she goes to a dance class. On Wednesday she goes to Lena's house, where Lena's mother is also at home. Sometimes she then goes to a drop-in center where she can get help with her homework. On Thursday, Jasmin comes home after school, and spends most of her time reading or sewing. Friday she comes home and talks on the telephone. She and her mother, Emilie, and younger brother then go out to eat when Emilie gets home from work at 6 p.m.

Although many children are inventive at finding ways to structure their time, others are not, and many become bored as they spend time that neither they, nor anyone else, has structured. Eric Holden spends several hours each afternoon at home, and he is generally by himself. Completing homework can be a problem.

> Sometimes I just can't concentrate. I just lie down and look at green leaves or count the people who walk by. That's very satisfying. In the summer I lie on the porch in the hammock. That's very pleasing. When I get depressed or in trouble that's what I do—look out the window.

Eric spends much of his time talking on the telephone with friends, and what he likes best about his after-school time is "talking to people. It's fun. If you talk to people [on the telephone] you don't have to visit them. That might be boring or take too much time." He also spends much of his time sleeping. He says, "I sleep as much as I can." What Eric likes least about his after-school time is "waking up, doing my chores, and when Mom gets upset."

Research on adolescent leisure indicates that developmentally appropriate leisure experiences have a level of difficulty sufficient to produce a feeling of challenge, without also producing anxiety in the adolescent. Insufficiently arousing, boring leisure time has been associated with deviant, high-risk behavior, alcohol use, smoking, and overeating (Caldwell, Smith, & Weissinger, 1992). The boring, unstructured time of several children in the present study is certainly a cause for concern.

TELEVISION

Watching television helps many children cope with boredom, fear, and loneliness, yet it can eat up time that is needed for more important pursuits and can leave children less active and engaged than they were before they turned on the set. Stanley Gates sometimes does not like the feeling of being alone in the house and says that when he is home alone, he sometimes feels a little nervous or frightened. When asked whether he has done anything about these problems to make them come out better, he answers.

"Watch TV . . . I don't think about it that much." He says his favorite time of day is after school because of "cartoons—why else?" As Bernice Gates sees it, "TV is a second mother to him."

Diana Hardy watches a good deal of television, too. As her mother notes, if she's alone and gets scared the television is company. But Tricia Hardy would rather have her daughter listen to radio. "I'm not against TV per se, but she watches it and she's a vegetable. It doesn't do a lot for her in a positive way." A year later, the situation has not changed:

> I try to help her with the TV by making it difficult to watch [hiding it in the closet]. I know that TV is comforting to have on when she's alone. If it's plugged in, the temptation is too great. She was really *addicted* to TV. She fought and manipulated the situation to keep watching. It was almost *insidious*.

Diana says she used to violate the television rule in her house. "I used to come straight home and watch cartoons. Then when I thought Mom was coming home I'd turn it off. She used to feel the back [of the television] and find out it was warm!" Diana says she follows the rules now.

Weining Chen is stricter about television when she is home with her daughters. When her daughters are home alone they are each allowed to watch two programs, "programs I approve like *Sesame Street*. But I know they watch more and not just the programs I allow. It is hard to stop them."

Zack Monroe, whose problems with self-discipline were described earlier, has a recurrent problem with the television. In the third year of the study, Zack was still having academic difficulties and was in danger of failing to graduate from eighth grade. After his most recent report card he cut the plug off the television set and put it away in his closet.

Computer games can serve the same functions and create the same problems as television. Eric Holden could not seem to limit his involvement even though his schoolwork suffered. Eventually, his mother removed the computer from the apartment. According to Eric, this tactic was effective:

> When I had the computer, my grades were low. Mom took it away last week. I've already seen improvement in a test I had last week. I don't like the system, but I've got to admit it works.

CONFLICTUAL AND NONSUPPORTIVE RELATIONSHIPS

Although the absence of others gives rise to many stressful challenges during the after-school hours, stress also arises from the unwanted presence of others. Deirdre Stevens often prefers to spend after-school time away from the house, now that her father works at home, because her older sister argues with him so much. Rebecca Myers spends two afternoons a week at home, and her stepfather, Sam, is generally there as well. Rebecca and Sam do not have a good relationship, and when Sam is in the house Rebecca often retreats to her own room. This, in turn, limits her options during the afternoon hours and contributes to her experience of boredom. Later in the study, Rebecca's mother says that Rebecca and Sam are "slowly working on their relationship." She attributes the change to the fact that Sam has stopped drinking and has begun attending Alcoholics Anonymous meetings.

Peers can also constitute a stressful unwanted presence. Julie Samuels was promoted directly from second grade to fourth grade. In her after-school program she feels she does not fit in comfortably with either the third graders or the fourth graders. Her mother complains that the after-school teachers do little to help Julie find a supportive set of friends. Later in the study, Julie leaves the program with her mother's blessing and begins spending afternoons at home or exchanging visits with two unsupervised girls who are her close friends. In this new situation she spends more time alone but feels less lonely than she had in the midst of her peers.

RESPONSIBILITY FOR OTHERS

Although the after-school hours offer some children freedom to pursue their own agendas, for others they require increased attention to the needs of others. As discussed earlier, children in low-income families and in single-parent households were particularly likely to become sibling caretakers.

Jasmin Perry is a big help to her mother, Emilie, on the home front. She picks up her younger brother, Leon, at the babysitter's on Fridays and on other days when Emilie is having "a rough day." As Emilie says, "I'm so tired when I get out of work. It really helps not to have to stop to pick up Leon. I can do groceries right after work on Fridays." Jasmin also does the breakfast dishes and any others she dirties during the day, folds laundry, takes care of her own room, and cleans the bathroom. According to Emilie, "sometimes she's great in doing everything I ask and more. I'll come home and the house will be spotless. Other times, she doesn't do a thing." In the second year of the study, Leon goes to school during the day, and Jasmin picks him up each afternoon after school and takes care of him until their mother returns from work.

MAKING SENSE OF AFTER-SCHOOL TIME

A final challenge many children face is finding meaning in the way they spend after-school time. All of the children in this study needed to come to terms with their parents' absence during the after-school hours and sometimes on into the evening and on weekends. Some had to explain to themselves their own heavy responsibilities, including sibling care. Others needed to make sense of their isolation or lack of freedom.

The children in low-income and single-parent families generally know very well that their mother's employment is necessary for their own subsistence, and they understand her absence from the home as crucial to their own economic well-being. When 10-year-old George Townsend was asked how he felt about his mother working, he said he liked it better, "so we have a roof over our heads and food." Diana Hardy also thinks it is good that her mother works. "We wouldn't have any money if she didn't work. She's been working or going to school all my life. I'm used to it." Dominique Nelson says her mother shows her she loves and cares about her in many ways. "She tells me. Gives me a kiss. And I know it. Still got a roof over my head."

In contrast, Carl Peters has difficulty understanding why his mother cannot spend after-school time with him. A school teacher, her work day coincides with his own. However, she stays on at the school to grade papers and plan the next day's lessons, tasks she accomplishes more efficiently at school than at home. Doing a good job of teaching is too important to her emotionally, she says, to make leaving school early a real option. Carl experiences her absence each afternoon as a puzzling rejection. Zack Monroe appreciates why his mother works so much, but regrets it just the same. "If she didn't work we'd be in trouble. She's dedicated. Sometimes you get lonely, I suppose." The long work hours of some parents with professional jobs may feel discretionary, not necessary, to children. They must then try to understand why their parents have voluntarily chosen to spend afternoon, evening, or weekend time without them.

SUMMARY

After-school hours can present children with a variety of challenges. Children who lack adult supervision may experience the temptation to relax or ignore household rules because no adult is present to enforce them. For many unsupervised children (and some with supervision) the lack of structure is felt most deeply and is experienced as boredom. Still other children feel overscheduled and wish for more "down" time. Children are sometimes frightened or lonely in their after-school settings. Although some children are challenged by the responsibility of caring for younger siblings, others must find a way to get along with children who are close in age, and still others cope with a lack of companionship. Making sense of their experiences and finding meaning in the ways they spend their time also constitute serious challenges for many children.

7

Social Relationships and Social Support

During the hours she spends each afternoon without adult supervision, Jasmin Perry is surrounded by extended family and family friends. She can visit her Aunt Margaret who lives downstairs ("she's always home"), as well as her Aunt Ann and Aunt Betty who live "across the yard." If these aunts are not home, she can always call her mother or father on the telephone. The Perry family has a tradition of mutual support. Emilie Perry's mother died when she was 5 years old, and the only mother she remembers is the aunt who left her nursing career to rear her and her five siblings. Emilie's father "went through a lot to keep us. He worked two jobs throughout my childhood." Emilie says that if she thinks Jasmin might be worried or sad about anything, "I try and talk to her. I tell her if she can't talk to me, she's got four aunts and a godmother down the street and she can talk to any of them."

Eleanor Townsend is grateful that she lives where she does, because her neighbors are able to help her sons out when they are on their own after school.

> One thing that's hard is they always have to have something to eat when they come home. They can't use the stove, so I have to have snacks they can make themselves. It makes it easier in this type of building [high rise public housing apartments] because I have so many friends and the boys have been raised here. If I leave a snack that has to be cooked, they can bring it to one of the neighbors to cook it for them.

When asked who her daughter can call or see after school when she is home alone, Terry Edwards mentions Cynthia's older brother, but aside from him, "Not a damn soul!" She later amends this to mention the man who runs a small local store who has made Cynthia feel welcome. Yet Terry finds that she has not added to her family's support systems in the year since her arrival in the community. She wonders why people are not more open and friendly, blaming it on the nature of city life.

Except in an emergency, 8-year-old Omar Jones cannot call or see other people when he is taking care of his younger brother and sister. Angela Jones is concerned that "by law Omar is too young to watch the kids." She is pleased that Omar is discrete. "He follows my directions. He doesn't tell people he's watching his siblings. He knows what goes on in here stays in here. We are a family. We keep our business in our house." Even Angela's mother does not know that Omar is sometimes responsible for the other children. "If she did, she wouldn't approve."

SOCIAL SUPPORT AND RESILIENCE

Children vary enormously in the supportive figures available to them during the after-school hours and at other times of day. Because after-school arrangements often challenge and even stress children, it becomes essential to understand the supportive relationships that help them cope with their after-school situations. As much research has demonstrated, stressful life experiences can lead to physical, emotional, and social problems for children, yet many children encountering even multiple and severe stresses escape disability (Rutter, 1979), and some actually emerge strengthened by their encounters with adversity (Elder, 1974; Fiske, 1982; Silverstein & Krate, 1975). Resources such as nurturance, companionship, assistance in problem solving, and reassurance of worth, conveyed through social relationships, can make the difference (Sandler, Miller, Short, & Wolchik, 1989; Werner & Smith, 1982).

NONPARENTAL ADULTS

Nonparental adults often assist parents in caring for children, and such assistance has been shown to protect the mental health and thus the supportive capacity of parents under stress, thus indirectly providing great benefits to children (Belle, 1982, Colletta, 1979; Crnic, Greenberg, Ragozin, Robinson, & Basham, 1983; Crockenburg, 1981; Weinraub & Wolf, 1983). Nonparental adults can also provide direct emotional and practical support to children. Zelkowitz (1982a) found that when mothers were stressed, depressed, or nonnurturant, children who received supportive care from other adults exhibited a reduced level of aggressive behavior in the home, in comparison to children who lacked such additional support. Wahler (1980) observed that on days marked by visits from supportive members of the mother's social network, both the mother and her children exhibited improved, positive social behavior to each other.

When parents are at work, children often have contact with babysitters, after-school teachers, coaches, neighbors, adult relatives, and other adults in their communities. These adults can provide companionship, direction, practical help, and emotional support that make a real difference to children. Although some children are fortunate enough to have a readily accessible support network, and other children are more isolated, it is also true that children react differently to the support opportunities they have. Some children take active steps to expand the circle of supportive people available to them after school, whereas others seem not to take advantage of potential support providers already close at hand.

Micah Somers probably did not start his after-school activities because of the people he would meet through them, but one result of his activities is an expanded circle of friends and supporters. When asked about the people with whom Micah has a special relationship, his mother includes his piano and dance teachers and his soccer coach, along with his classroom teachers. As his mother sees it, Micah "looks up to these people. They treat him nicely and are proud of him, so he performs well for them. They are kind and patient, and give him positive reinforcement for both the work he does and the person he is." Micah names his teacher, and his soccer, baseball, and basketball coaches as support providers. These people can usually figure out if Micah is feeling worried or sad, and Micah usually tells them if he is upset about something.

Carl Peters has a small family, and in the first year of the study he reports receiving minimal support from those family members he does have. In the second year of the study, however, when Carl is 12, his support network expands substantially with the addition of a girlfriend, Bonnie. Not only is Bonnie important to him, but her grandmother, aunt, and uncle are all at home in the afternoon and therefore available to Carl after school. According to Carl's mother, Bonnie's family seems to like Carl very much. Bonnie's mother is "kind and nice to him" and he "talks to her about stuff." Bonnie's dad "kids around" with Carl. Carl's mother believes her son likes them because they are the kind of family he would like to have himself. During the year in which Carl's social world expands to include Bonnie and her family, Carl is not only more satisfied with the way he spends his time after school, but he seems to feel more positive about himself and other people in general. In the next year of the study Carl and Bonnie break up, and his assessments and descriptions become somewhat more negative once again.

There are other people nearby on whom Zack Monroe can call or whom he can see after school, including an elderly lady who lives in their apartment building and who is, according to Zack's mother, like "a second grandmother" to him, and another neighbor who is a teacher and is home in the afternoon. But Zack is usually not home in the afternoon anyway. "He usually only goes over to their house if he has lost his keys." Peggy hired a math tutor for Zack when he was failing that subject and in danger of not graduating from eighth grade. But Zack was always late for his appointments, and the tutor was expensive and "just not helping at all," so they abandoned this attempt to provide Zack additional support. Peggy often considers hiring someone to be with Zack when he comes home from school, but she questions whether it would be possible to find the right person to stay at the apartment. She wonders if Zack would come home even if someone were there for him.

After a year of afternoons spent mostly alone at home, doing homework and chores, drawing, watching television, and talking with friends on the telephone, 10-year-old Irene Castillo decides to offer her services two afternoons a week as a volunteer in the counselor's office at school. Not only does she gain the company of a supportive adult, but she finds meaning through participating in useful work. Eleven-year-old Bonita Moore babysits and takes a job at a day-care center, where she develops close relationships with the babies for whom she cares and with her adult colleague. Michelle Kelley sometimes stays after school to help her teacher clean up after classes. Cynthia Edwards often fills the hour or so between the end of the school day and the start of her weekly gymnastics class by helping out the school librarian.

SIBLINGS

When parents are away at work, brothers and sisters are the family members most often available to share after-school time. Sibling relationships are often high in conflict, yet siblings can and do support each other in crucial ways, most often by providing companionship (Furman & Buhrmester, 1985). Older siblings are frequent sources of instrumental aid, and same-gender siblings, particularly those close in age, often provide emotional intimacy (Furman & Buhrmester, 1985). Some studies suggest a special supportiveness from older sisters (Blyth & Foster-Clark, 1987; Bryant, 1985), yet in Furman and Buhrmester's (1985) research, brothers provided more instrumental aid to their siblings than did sisters.

The sibling relationship is particularly important when children face difficult life circumstances. Sandler (1980) found that older siblings provided a protective buffer to low-income children experiencing stressful life events. Kempton, Armistead, Wierson, and Forehand (1991) discovered that, in divorced families, adolescents with siblings evidenced fewer behavioral problems than did only children. Among children living with married parents who were high in conflict, those with close sibling relationships showed fewer adjustment problems than children without close sibling relationships (Jenkins, 1992). Recently, Caya and Liem (1998) found that sibling support in childhood is associated with greater adjustment in adulthood among those who grew up in high-conflict homes. In line with this research on the supportive potential of sibling relationships, Long and Long (1982) found that children who spent unsupervised time at home with siblings were less likely to develop high levels of fear and sleep disturbances than unsupervised children at home alone.

Little is known of the particular experiences of children cared for by older siblings while parents are away, or of the experiences of the sibling caretakers. Bryant's (n.d.) research has shown that sibling caretaking is relatively unskilled in comparison to parental caretaking. Younger siblings report that older siblings are more scolding and physically punitive than either mothers or fathers, whereas mothers and fathers demonstrate more nurturance, protectiveness, control, and consistency, promote more autonomy, responsibility, and achievement, and provide more discipline and companionship than do siblings.

In accord with research on the conflictual character of many sibling relationships and the relatively unskilled nature of much sibling caretaking, Berman et al. (1992) found that children cared for after school by older siblings reported significantly more negative self-concepts than children cared for after school by adults or children in self-care.

Yet Woods (1972) discovered that children with extensive household responsibilities, including sibling care, actually excelled in many achievement and intelligence tests. The "required helpfulness" of the sibling caretaker role seems to promote resilience in children under stress (Werner, 1990). For children growing up in high-risk families, involvement in sibling caretaking, either as provider or recipient, proved to be a major protective factor (Werner, 1990).

Michelle and Nate Kelley spend some unsupervised time together in each of the years of the study and illustrate both the companionship and the conflict that are so characteristic of sibling relationships. According to their mother, Michelle and Nate are both often at home at the same time,

> but they are not necessarily together. It is more parallel. They both have their own friends over and are usually in different parts of the house. I don't know that they are becoming closer, but they are getting along better than they used to.

In the first year of the study, when Michelle is 9 and Nate is 11, what Michelle does not like about her after-school arrangement is "when I fight with my brother. He's bigger and stronger than me and there's no one to tell him to stop. It's also quite lonely." Michelle thinks some of her friends have more fun than she does after school, "because a lot of time they have people to play with and their parents are home and they don't have a big brother to pick on them." That same year, Nate states that his preferred after-school arrangement would be to "not have my sister at home." However, in discussing the people who are most important to him he mentions Michelle as the one person he just likes to be with when he is worried or sad, even if he does not talk about what is upsetting him, "because she's a good person to be around. She understands me."

Their mother, Jane, thinks that when the children disagree

> they yell and storm around. Nate throws things, storms up to his room and locks himself in. "Actually, it is a microcosm of what happens when [my husband] and I fight. They both go off in their separate directions."

When asked if their arguments ever turn physical, Jane first says, "no," but then notes that once, in the previous year, Michelle locked Nate out of the house.

> Nate kicked the door in and broke it. She says she locked him out because he was going to hit her. He denies it and says he knocked the door in because he had to go to the bathroom and she wouldn't let him in.

Timothy Kelley agrees that Michelle and Nate's arguments sometimes do turn physical.

> Michelle will call me and say Nate hit her. She'll call me and say he's being a pain in the ass and ask me to talk to him, which I will. In the past I would get three or four calls in a row.

In the third year of the study, Jane reports the children's arguments as diminishing over time. She sees their arguments as arising because

> Michelle is more socially adept than Nate is. She has always had more friends than Nate has had. Until this year, Nate has usually just had one friend at a time. In the past, Nate used to try and horn in on Michelle and her friends. This year, Nate has two friends, and he is getting better at setting up his own social situations. Michelle is beginning to see that having an older brother can be an asset socially. One of her friends has a crush on Nate. Also, Michelle is feeling good about herself this year, mainly because of a special relationship she has developed with one of her teachers. She doesn't seem to feel she has to "knock off number one" anymore.

Timothy sees his children as developing a closer relationship over time as a result of the hours they spend together after school. "They might bug each other, but they get along okay. I don't know how much of their after-school time is spent together, but they will look out for each other." Over the years of the study, Nate and Michelle consistently named each other as support providers, especially as people with whom they have fun.

In the Somers household there is some disagreement about whether Vanessa is "in charge" when she is home alone with Micah, who is 2 years younger. Laura Somers says:

> I don't really think of it as Vanessa being in charge. I leave separate lists for both of them. For example: Vanessa—do homework, practice piano, eat your salad, make so and so for supper. They can check things off and when I come home, even if they're in bed, I can see what has happened, what they did and didn't do.

Micah agrees and thinks that "no one takes care of each other." But Vanessa says she has to tell Micah to do his homework and do things like practice the piano and eat his vegetables. As she sees it, "I'm in charge."

Despite this area of disagreement, both children describe a close and supportive relationship with minimal quarreling over the duration of the study. Micah says that he thinks he and Vanessa have always been very close. "When we're home we usually each do our own thing, but if we have problems we talk. [We] might make dinner together." Laura says that an advantage for Vanessa of being with Micah after school is "it makes her responsible for her brother. He looks up to her." For both Vanessa and Micah, time alone together "gives them both time to share, to get to know each other, to share ideas without Mom and Dad being there." She believes it is reassuring for both of them. Peter says that Vanessa and Micah are "very close. They play together, help each other, and are involved with each other's play and activities. Micah will check with Vanessa for advice and to verify things." Peter sees Vanessa as "nurturing and supportive" with Micah. As he says in a later interview, "Vanessa is his mentor." Micah does not think he is getting closer to Vanessa because of being home with her after school. "I don't think it changes it. We'd be close anyway." Nor does he think they get in more fights because they are sometimes home alone together. "No. If we get in fights, they're not serious. They last only 10 minutes. We don't hold grudges."

Cynthia Edwards does not think she is getting closer to her older brother because of the time they spend at home together after school. "No," she says, "he's always on the telephone." From their mother's perspective, the basis of their relationship is "proximity. They're both here. Other than that, they don't have a lot in common." (Craig is 7 years older than Cynthia.) In a later interview, Terry says that Craig "is adored. He can do little wrong. He is good with her but doesn't make enough time for her. Cynthia is very thoughtful of him, but he doesn't reciprocate a lot."

SIBLING CARETAKING

Over the course of the study, more than one third of the children who lived with siblings experienced a regular sibling caretaking relationship in the absence of adult supervision. Several of the children in the study had extensive after-school responsibility for substantially younger siblings. Although conflicts often arose, and caretaker siblings sometimes regretted the opportunities they lost because of their caretaking responsibilities, the relationships between younger siblings and their caretakers generally seemed quite strong. Occasionally, a sibling caretaker did not seem ready for the responsibility.

Meiguei Chen began taking care of her younger sister, Lian, when Meiguei was 9 years old and Lian was 5. At first, the two girls spent several hours each day in the children's room of the public library. Meiguei believes that this time together brought them closer. "At the library she [Lian] is quieter than at home. I learn more about her." The next year, the girls continued to spend after-school time together, but in their own home. Lian can be an obstacle to Meiguei's social life. "Sometimes my friends ask me to go to their house after school, but I have to say no, because who would take care of my sister?" Despite this, and despite their arguing "all the time," their mother believes they are developing a closer relationship because of the time they spend together after school. Meiguei agrees. "We always play games, and during the games she'll say, 'Oh, do you know what happened today?'"

Emilie Perry believes that her daughter, Jasmin, does not mind taking care of her brother, Leon, "but sometimes he aggravates her." Emilie thinks they were closer when Leon was a baby. "Now he's independent. As long as she can help them and do for them she likes kids as babies." Jasmin does not believe her time alone together with Leon is bringing them closer, "'cause we mostly get into fights." As their mother sees it,

> all those two do is squawk among themselves. . . . They'll be all lovey-dovey until the next one. She'll tell him on school vacation days he can stay with her. They'll make it through half the day. By the time I get home she'll say he's never staying with her again.

Yet Jasmin also appreciates the importance of Leon in her life. According to Jasmin, Emilie has told the children "we have to stay together through life 'cause if she's not there, we'll always be there for each other." And, Jasmin adds, "I believe that." When asked if there are people she just likes to be with when she is worried or sad, Jasmin names her mother and Leon, "'cause they're people I love."

Ms. Townsend also values closeness between her two sons. "I'm not going to have any more children, so it's important for them to be close." When her older son, George, complained about having to watch his younger brother, Michael, she explained to him "that we were a family, and that was the only way we could make it together." Her perception, and that of the two boys, is that they are becoming closer as a result of the time they spend together after school. In the second year of the study, with George in a program for academically talented students, Michael goes to a babysitter in the housing project until George can look after him. George must forego the organized sports at which he excels. Instead, he returns from school and completes his homework as quickly as he can and then brings Michael home. George realizes that Michael does not like being with the babysitter and that he "wants to come home early because there's lots of kids there, so I come home to pick him up." Michael, in turn, says that George teaches him a lot of things, like how to pitch and play basketball, "and I learn about him." Both boys name each other as important support providers and rate the time they spend together positively.

Weiss (1974) argued that those who take responsibility for the well-being of a child can find meaning in their own lives through the sense of being needed, the opportunity to nurture another. Many of the sibling caretakers in this study appeared to derive such meaning, even when their responsibilities also imposed sacrifices.

FRIENDS

During the school years, children's capacities for friendship with peers grow markedly. With greater age, children are better able to realize what is unique in another child and increasingly able to recognize and meet a peer's need for social support (Youniss, 1980). Over time, the children in this study tended to name an increasing number of friends as providers of social support.

The importance to children of particular friends their own age was also revealed in their eagerness to spend after-school time with them. When asked about the after-school arrangements they desired, children most often expressed a wish to visit with their friends. This was frequently difficult because children might attend different after-school programs, or one child might attend a program, while another went home after school. Unsupervised children might not be allowed to have friends visit, or their friends' parents might not allow the friends to visit the unsupervised child, or the logistics of transporting children who lived at some distance might rule out the possibility of after-school visits. George Townsend, for instance, would like to spend more time with several of his friends after school, but he can't, "because we go to different schools, and Robert has two homes, one with his grandmother a 20-minute ride away from here." Despite their interest in spending after-school time with friends, only one fourth of the children in the study spend most of their time after school with their close friends. One third of the children rarely see their best friends after school, and the remaining children spend some time, but less than half of their after-school time, with close friends.

For Bertha Martell, changes in the friendship patterns at her after-school program are central to her after-school experience. When we asked her if she thought some of her friends had more fun than she did after school she replied:

> Yes, indeed! Because I used to play with Nikki, but now Nikki has left the after school and now Esther and Lori play with Cass and I don't have anybody to play with [at the after-school]. But I just hang upside down on the bars [of the jungle gym].

When Adam Stone was 11 he told us what he liked best about being on his own after school was, "I get to play with other friends." The next year, he told us he would like to go to an after-school program because, "I'd like to be with my friends."

Over the course of the study, rearrangements of after-school time were often designed to allow children to spend time with their friends. One reason Julie Samuels left her after-school program was her lack of friends there. Having skipped a grade, she did not fit in well with either the children in her new class or the children in the class she had left. Her mother says she was often alone and unengaged at the after-school program. After switching to an unsupervised arrangement, including two afternoons a week at home alone, two afternoons at a friend's house, and one afternoon on which a different friend visits her, Julie is happier and less lonely than she was the year before, surrounded by same-age peers who were not her particular friends.

Julie's mother is delighted about the days Julie spends at her friend's house but wishes Julie did not have to be home alone two afternoons a week. She believes that when alone Julie is more likely to be lonely and to worry if her mother is late returning from work. Julie sometimes copes with loneliness by pretending there is another person with her. "Like I take out a game for two people and start playing for that person."

Julie also mentions that her own activities are different on days she spends with friends. Julie watches television much of the time she is home alone, but with friends she is more likely to ride her bicycle or go running. In this respect, her experience accords with the children surveyed by Medrich et al. (1982). These children overwhelmingly reported that they liked to do more physically active things when they were with their friends. Only when alone were these children likely to engage in sedentary activities.

Micah Somers is blessed with a large group of readily available friends he can play with when there is a lull in his busy schedule of after-school activities. His family lives on a dead-end street that abuts the school park, and many of Micah's friends live only a short distance away. "There are always kids in the park playing, or my friends live only a few minutes away." Micah sees each of his six best friends after school as well as during the school day.

> I like having free time after school to play with friends and all and I like in the spring when I have lots of activities [soccer, baseball, dancing, piano] but it's sort of nice to be free and do whatever you want.

Micah does comment that it is sometimes difficult to be with only his best friends in a small group. "One thing that's strange. If I try to play with my friends [I have a lot of friends, we hang out in a crowd of 10 or so], it's hard to just be with a few of them." In an even more ideal world, Micah would like time to be with one or two chosen friends as well as time to spend with his whole crowd.

Although good friends can add zest to school afternoons, and although they are often an effective antidote to loneliness, boredom, and fear, they are not a panacea and they can bring with them new problems. At 14, Gregory

Polansky spends most of his after-school time "hanging out" with his four closest friends. Yet Gregory rates the time he spends this way as negatively as possible. He even gives his part-time job a higher rating. Gregory complains that there is little to do in the town where they live, except go to fast food restaurants. Even the presence of his close friends does not turn their time together into something positive and engaging.

Micah Somers' mother believes that telephone conversations with friends are a needless distraction for Micah.

> He is not allowed to talk on the phone. I think it is a waste of time and he has too much homework. It has only been a problem since he discovered girls. Also he has a friend who has a conference phone. They have three way conversations and they'll stay on the phone for hours. He doesn't have time for that.

Ms. Somers thinks that Micah would like to play with his friends everyday, as well as participate in activities like sports and dancing. But, "homework has to be done and there are time constraints. Micah and his sister have other commitments."

More dramatically, Eric Holden got in trouble cutting school and stealing from cars with his close friend. In response, Eric's mother prohibited him from seeing or talking to this boy. Rhonda Stiles allows her son, Justin, to go to his friend's house after school, but does not allow Justin's friend to visit him. Rhonda fears that in Justin's house the friend will get her son into trouble because it is not his own home that is at risk. Bernice Gates is skeptical about many of her son's friends, believing that "a couple of them are good kids, but most of them are trouble."

Yet, sometimes friends can actually protect children from misbehavior. Frank Latimore's friends are very important to him, precisely because they help him regulate his own impulses and stay out of trouble. According to Frank, "A friend will stop you from doing the wrong thing."

Although children are born into families, they choose their own friends, and thus have some control over the characteristics of these friends. Children who are cautious and rule abiding typically have similar friends, and children who are attracted to risk and to rule breaking may well be attracted to friends with similar predilections. In the middle of the study, Zack Monroe succeeds in being accepted by a new group of friends, the "in" crowd, to which Zack has aspired. These friends do not inspire great confidence in Zack's mother, however, who much prefers the less popular but probably more trustworthy friends he previously had.

Even when an individual child might stay away from risky or antisocial behavior, a group of children together may egg each other on, encouraging rule breaking and misbehavior. Parents weigh the dangers friends bring along with their potential to provide companionship and emotional support to children in the after-school hours.

PETS

For children who feel lonely on their own, pets can be important sources of support (Bryant, 1985; Guerney, 1991; Long & Long, 1982). Furman (1989) found that the fourth-grade children he studied turned frequently to their pets for companionship, a sense of reliable alliance, intimacy, and, especially, opportunities to provide nurturance. The children reported providing more nurturance to their pets than to anyone else in their networks. Although pets recede in importance among older, seventh-grade children, Furman noted that pets are significant support figures to the younger children in his study.

Diana Hardy likes cuddling with her kittens and "they lick me and they're really nice." Something that made Diana feel happy in the day or two before our last interview with her was "my kitten doing silly little things like hanging on my robe." When Diana feels afraid that someone might break into the house when she is home alone, her mother often suggests that she cuddle the cats or go to Ms. Hardy's room, where she feels safer. Diana says her cats have "personalities" and "you can play with them different." Also, they won't tell secrets that you tell them. Diana says that she always has someone to talk to, because if there is no one to talk to, "I can always talk to my cat." She lists feeding her cats as the first thing she does when she comes home from school. Acknowledging the importance of these pets, Diana and her mother chose the name of her favorite cat as the code name for their family in our study. Vanessa Somers says, "When you're sad, cats can sit on your lap." Cynthia Edwards thinks of the cat at her father's house as a special friend. "He's furry and always warm. He loves you. He gives me playful swats. He never puts his claws out when he touches me." Michael Townsend has a rabbit at his father's house, where his baby sister takes care of it. Michael considers the rabbit a special friend. "He likes to jump with me. He likes to play with me."

Eric Holden had several exotic pets, and two of these, an iguana and a bird, died during the week before our first interviews with the Holden family. According to Jessica Holden, Eric was upset and felt guilty that he was not taking care of his animals right.

> He was crying when he found the iguana was dead and he wanted to sleep in my bed. He said he couldn't handle the responsibility, and that the iguana used to make him feel better.

Eric told the interviewer that he used to just sit and watch his pet iguana, before it died. This was pleasing because the iguana never said, "go away, kid." In a later year of the study, Eric mentions that he often pretends that this pet iguana is still on his shoulder. Zack Monroe thinks of his cat as a special friend, even a member of the family. One year, Zack says, "He never puts me down, is always there, always seems to understand." In the final year of the study he says his cat is "the only one who seems to really understand."

For some children, even stuffed animals provide support. Cynthia Edwards, for instance, describes several stuffed animals and dolls as playmates who keep her company and cheer her up when she is lonely, bored, or scared. She finds particular comfort in the stuffed animal her absent father gave her. When she worries that there are monsters in her closet, she talks to this stuffed animal and "he scares my problems away." She asks the interviewer, "You know why I love him so much? Because he's from my daddy."

PARENTAL SUPPORT

Parents, of course, are crucial support providers to children. For fifth and sixth graders, parents are the most frequently named sources of affection, reliable alliance, enhancement of worth, and instrumental aid (Furman & Buhrmester, 1985). Mothers are primary sources of nurturance and intimacy throughout the school years and well into adolescence (Belle & Longfellow, 1983; Kon & Losenkov, 1978; Youniss & Smollar, 1985). Children who report positive relationships with their mothers have been found to have high academic achievement and personality adjustment (Woods, 1972), and children who frequently confide in their mothers report higher levels of self-esteem and internal locus of control than children who do not confide so frequently (Belle & Longfellow, 1984). During the Great Depression children whose families experienced severe economic losses and those whose fathers treated them with hostility still showed positive psychological outcomes when their mothers were nurturant and loving (Elder, Caspi, & Van Nguyen, 1986). Positive father–child relationships are also associated with high self-esteem, internal locus of control, intellectual development, and satisfactory peer relations (Biller, 1976). For children of divorce, a good relationship with the noncustodial parent is associated with good adjustment (Wallerstein & Kelly, 1980). A positive relationship with at least one parent has been identified as a protective factor that buffers children from the potentially adverse effects of marital discord, parental mental illness, and social disadvantage (Rutter, 1979). In line with such findings, Long and Long (1983) reported that children who have close relationships with their parents appear less likely than those with more distant relationships to develop intense fears when they are without adult supervision.

CONTACT WITH PARENTS DURING WORKING HOURS

Although the children in the present study do not routinely spend their after-school hours with their parents, many children do contact parents by telephone and several visit them at work. Bonita Moore visits each of her parents about once or twice a week. Zack Monroe can easily visit his mother at work, and does so two or three times a week, even though she find these visits disruptive. Eleanor Townsend says she generally calls her sons once a day from work, and they generally call her three times each afternoon. The frequency of Eric Holden's calls to his mother varies from day to day. "Sometimes I only call her two times a day. Sometimes I call her 15 times. Sometimes I ask her to call me in one half hour."

Children typically find these calls and visits with parents important, and both parents and children are often troubled when workplace rules or logistics prevent such contacts from taking place. Diana Hardy cannot reach her mother after school by telephone, so Tricia Hardy calls Diana. "I like to talk to her within one half hour after she's come home from school." Bill MacCarthy is forced by his supervisor to limit his calls home to one a day. Early in the afternoon, Suzanne Peters' sons can reach her by telephone at the elementary school where she teaches, but once the secretaries have left for the day there is no one to answer the office telephone and then come to her classroom to alert her that there is a call. Because of this limitation, her sons were not able to reach her when Carl broke his arm playing basketball. They made their way to the hospital without her. Terry Edwards works the midnight shift, and would like to speak with her daughter just as Cynthia gets out of bed in the early morning. Unfortunately, that is also her busiest time at work, which makes calling home then difficult.

Over half of the children in the study were frequent callers or visitors to parents' workplaces, and most of the remaining children could call or visit at least one of their parents at work and did so at least occasionally.

These findings offer a more optimistic view of parent–child contact after school than those of Seligson et al. (1990), who surveyed the parents of somewhat younger children in the city of Boston. They found that almost one half of the employed women in their survey could not call their children from work or receive calls from their children, even in an emergency. The parents Seligson and her colleagues surveyed had somewhat lower family incomes and substantially less education, on average, than the parents of our sample, and this may explain the discrepancies between the two studies. The employed mothers whom Seligson and her colleagues surveyed reported considerable inflexibility at work: One third could not take time off from work when their children were ill, almost two thirds could not take time off for school holidays or early dismissal days, and fewer than half reported having any say at all in their own work schedules. Furthermore, employed fathers reported similar problems. Flexibility on the job was associated with higher income positions, so that low- and moderate-income parents were least likely to be able to adjust their work schedules or take calls from their children.

Telephone talks with parents feel highly supportive to many children. When Meiguei Chen has a bad day, she calls her mother at work to talk with her about it, and these conversations are helpful to her. Michelle Kelley says she sometimes get scared when she gets telephone calls at home. She does not want the callers to know she is home alone. But, afterward she calls her parents, and "it's really comforting." Yet Michelle's parents put some limits on her freedom to call them at work. "If I call them a lot, like when I fight with my brother, they tell me not to call unless it's an emergency."

Although calls from parents feel supportive to many children, to others they do not. Angela Jones, whose 8-year-old son, Omar, is sometimes at home alone with his younger siblings, says she responds to her own anxieties by telephoning home frequently. She recounts a recent, typical telephone call.

Mother: "Is everything all right?"
Omar: "Yes, Mommy. Is Daddy on his way home?"
Mother: "Yes, Daddy should be home soon."
Omar: "I'm hanging up now."
Mother: "No, wait! What are the kids doing? Let me talk to your brother. [Talks to Christopher]. Is the baby hungry? Her bottle is in the fridge. Daddy will be home soon."

I call home like crazy," Angela says, "but Omar doesn't like this." The calls provide Angela some reassurance, but do not provide Omar with the supportive resources he needs in his difficult situation. In this way, they are somewhat reminiscent of the nighttime visits Terry Edwards makes from work to home just to reassure herself that her children are all right.

PARENTAL SUPPORT DURING NONWORKING HOURS

Most of the children in this study report close and supportive relationships with parents. When asked about the people who provide them with five different social support resources, most children name their mothers as providers of four or five. When asked to rate the quality of time they spend with members of their social networks, most children give time they spend with their mothers the highest possible or next-to-highest rating. Children's ratings for their fathers are only slightly less positive, which is particularly impressive because many of the children in the study do not live with their fathers and some have virtually no contact with their fathers. It may be that in some cases children idealize time with rarely seen fathers. Yvonne Hayes, for instance, says in an early interview that she gets sad when she thinks about her father because she has not seen him since she was 2 years old. In the first 3 years of the study Sandra Hayes says that Yvonne never sees her father, although in the final year of the study this changes to "almost never." In that year, Yvonne rates the quality of time with her father at the highest possible level, giving time with him a higher rating than time with her mother.

Even though the parents in this study generally could not be with their children during the after-school hours, most successfully communicated their love, caring, and concern. Jason Lehman's mother puts notes in his lunch box so she can convey her love even when they are apart. When they are together she hugs and kisses Jason, tells him she loves him, buys him little presents, and finds ways of doing things with him that are fun for both of them. When Diana Hardy tells her mother she feels afraid to be alone in the house, Tricia often suggests that Diana go to Tricia's room. Just being in her mother's room reassures Diana and reduces her anxiety.

Emilie Perry shows her love for her daughter in a variety of ways, including letting Jasmin sleep in her bed.

> I feel bad I'm away most of the day and all we have are the nights together. I tell her I love her, I talk to her, I hug her. I tell her that whatever I'm doing, I'm doing because I love her. I'm not going to hurt her and I'm not going to let anyone else hurt her.

According to Emilie,

> My kids aren't neglected. If I can't do something with them, I find someone who can. Jasmin likes to have people over for dinner, and she likes to help me prepare everything. My friends and I sometimes have pajama parties with all our kids. Sometimes my friends and I will take all the kids window shopping, like at Christmas time, and we have a lot of fun.

Jane Kelley says her 11-year-old son, Nate, is "tactile defensive," and does not allow a lot of touching, but likes his hair to be played with. His sister, Michelle, likes hugs. Michelle says that when she is worried or sad her mom hugs her "and I feel good." Gregory Polansky's father rejects kissing and hugging as a way to show his son love and concern. "I don't believe in it or don't do it, anyway." But he shows his love in other ways. "I yell at him. 'Don't do this. Don't do that. You have to watch out for this or that.' It's not really yelling, it's teaching, preaching." Gregory, however, does not see this behavior as supportive and says that his father does "nothing" to let him know he loves him and cares for him.

According to Laura Somers, evenings in their household are rushed, but mornings, when Micah is getting ready for school, "that is when I read to him." They can also talk together and enjoy being together on the occasions when Laura is home in the afternoons, or taking him places in the car, or on the weekends. In the Kelley family, the two children gravitate to their parents in the evening hours, and their parents respond to them. As Jane Kelley describes it, "They do their homework around the dining room table. They tend to want to be around us, to follow us around, to float around us and want to talk."

Meiguei Chen says that evening is her favorite time of day, because "then my mom picks me up and she brings me home." In the evenings, Meiguei, her 5-year-old sister, Lian, and their mother are almost always together in the living room. Weining teaches Meiguei math and Chinese, and they play and watch television together. Weining says Meiguei tells her about her day "as soon as I see her. Then she never stops talking." If Weining thinks Meiguei might be worried or sad about something, "I hold her, talk to her, pat her." To show Meiguei she loves her and cares about her, "we sit or lie together on the sofa. They [her daughters] like to be on my body." Meiguei says that the things her mother does to let her know she loves her and cares about her are, "kisses and hugs me, and tells me nice things about me." Her father, she says, "gives me nice things. Tells me nice things about myself. Keeps telling me to be happy, just have fun, be yourself." Meiguei rates the time she spends with both her parents as highly as possible, seeing her mother in particular as a source of many forms of social support.

FLUCTUATIONS IN PARENTAL SUPPORT

Parental support to children may decline when parents themselves are stressed, depressed, or demoralized (Longfellow, Zelkowitz, & Saunders, 1982; Weissman & Paykel, 1974; Zelkowitz, 1982b). The tribulations of unpleasant or demanding work (Piotrkowski, 1978), the difficulties of single-parent lifestyles (Weiss, 1979), and the oppression of racism and poverty (Silverstein & Krate, 1975), can lead parents to withdraw emotional support from children. Parents whose children must become responsible and independent at a young age may also try to discourage the child's emotional dependency on adults, believing that such support "spoils" children and leaves them dangerously vulnerable in a world where others will not be so supportive or nurturant (Jeffers, 1967; Nightingale, 1993; Silverstein & Krate, 1975).

Peggy Monroe faces considerable stress at work, and the combination of this stress and her difficulties with Zack are taking their toll.

> I've been working so hard. I'd never encourage anyone to have a child alone. I just don't have the energy to deal with things. Sometimes I come home from work, tired and worn out, and I walk into the house and see he hasn't done anything—I come into my room and close the door. I'm feeling angry and depressed and Zack knows enough just to stay away.

This pattern is a painful one for both Zack and Peggy. Zack misses his mother when she is away, and in her absence he often seems incapable of completing the tasks that are required of him. His repeated failures to meet his mother's expectations have a demoralizing effect on her, particularly when she is already exhausted from a long day at work. This demoralization, in turn, leads to her withdrawal, depriving Zack of what he most needs and wants: his mother's engaged attention. Without that attention, his own demoralization makes it still more difficult to live up to the standards his mother holds.

When Zack was 13, his mother took a new job with substantially shorter hours and much less stress. She is now generally home by 6 p.m., although she still has an occasional evening meeting and sometimes works part of a weekend. (Zack mentions the shorter hours to his interviewer, but emphasizes that his mother is still sometimes out past 6 p.m.). Because of Peggy's shorter work hours, she and Zack are able to have more evening time together, evenings Zack generally spends struggling with his homework. If Zack completes his homework, Peggy reads Gulliver's Travels to him. "He likes to be read to. I've been reading to him all his life, just about."

Sharon Cole describes how easily misunderstandings can arise when she is distracted by her own troubles. On one occasion, after having a "bad day," she picked Brian up from school. He had also had a bad day, and his foot was hurting, but because of her own preoccupations she was not "tuned in" to this. They stopped to pick up Brian's younger sister at her day care center, and Sharon asked Brian to go in and get her. He said, "No." Sharon said, all right, she would get her. Again, Brian said, "No." His mother asked then what he did want, and Brian said he wanted them both to go in together. When Sharon asked why, he responded, "I just need to hang on you for a while."

Sharon also reveals that her son is sensitive in offering her support when she is distressed. She describes one incident that took place just 3 weeks after her divorce from Brian's father had been finalized. Sharon was talking on the telephone and started crying. Brian came in and wanted to know why. Sharon said she was all right, and Brian could talk to her after the call. When the call ended, Brian summoned his mother into his room in a manner identical to hers when she wants to talk to one of the children. He said, "Now, you know there's nothing you can't talk to me about. Why are you so upset?" Sharon told him, "After a divorce people feel very sensitive and get upset easily. I was upset, but I am really fine.

What I am feeling is no different from how you feel when you've had an argument with someone. I really am fine." Brian asked her why she was rocking back and forth on the bed. She said she sometimes rocked when she was upset. For 5 years she'd had babies to rock, and no one knew whether she was upset. But she didn't have anyone to rock anymore. Brian said, "Yes, you do." He got up from where he was sitting and went over and sat in his mother's lap so she could rock him.

Rhonda Stiles tries to protect Justin from own work-related stress, and especially from the misperception that her stressed behavior reflects a problem with Justin. When she has had a hard day at work, she explains that if she gets edgy it is not his fault, it's that she needs to unwind. "Even if there's an argument between the parents I tell him it has nothing to do with him, because he thinks, 'maybe it's me.'"

Layla Williams' mother, who works as many as 100 hours per week, has little time to spend with her daughter. When asked whether there are certain times of day she and Layla are most likely to talk together or just enjoy being together, Jocelyn replies,

> Not really. During the day they're in school. When they come home, I'm going out. Maybe on Saturdays. But Layla's at the age now where really we don't spend time together. She's used to my not being here. We're not a close-knit family.

Just as she carefully shapes their behaviors, Jocelyn teaches her children how to respond emotionally to life. When Jocelyn is asked by the interviewer, "Can you generally tell when Layla has had a bad day?" she hesitates. "Sometimes," she says. "She doesn't have too many bad days. I try to explain to them how to deal with bad days. There's always something good that happens on a bad day." Although Jocelyn will take Layla aside and ask her what's troubling her if she sees Layla looking down, she also tries to teach Layla to look at the bright side of things and not allow herself to become saddened when things don't go just right. Self-reliance is of paramount importance to Jocelyn, and even in the realm of emotional comforting, Jocelyn wants her daughter to be able to take care of herself.

In training her children so rigorously, Jocelyn believes she is also showing her love for them, and this is how Layla sees it. When asked what things her mother does to let her know she loves her and cares for her, Layla says, "she tells me to go to the store for her. She tells me to get good grades at school. She asks me to clean my room, so I can show her I can do it by myself." Layla names her mother as a provider of all of the social support resources we ask about and rates the time she does spend with her mother as highly as possible.

CHILDREN'S UTILIZATION OF SUPPORT

Parental provision of support is complicated in the adolescent years if, as often happens, children withdraw from parents and become impatient with parental companionship and displays of affection. Several parents reported that children who had actively sought to spend time with their parents in earlier years now look forward more to time spent apart. In the final year of the study, Clara Shepard is usually at home when her son returns from school, but he generally spends time elsewhere. According to Clara, Max "really does not want to be with me this year." As Max sees it, "rules have been fed to me since I was younger. No one has to tell them to me even though my mom does sometimes—she's neurotic." Mary Ellen Kelliher, who used to enjoy spending time with her mother, now wishes her mother worked every day "until midnight."

Peggy Monroe does not see as much of Zack on the weekends as she did when he was younger. He often spends Friday or Saturday at a friend's house. "We have gotten out of the habit of going to see movies together. He is getting to an age where he is just spending most of his time with his friends. He doesn't sit with me at the movies anymore even when we do go."

Stacey Moore says her family is very affectionate. "We'll always say, 'I love you,' and hugs and kisses are part of the routine." But when her daughter, Barbara, is 15, Stacey says "This year is a little different. I don't know why. It's not as easy. Barbara doesn't always want to be hugged and kissed." Barbara's younger sister, Bonita, "will still let the hugs and kisses happen, spontaneously."

When Eric Holden is 14 his mother reports that, "As he grows older we spend less and less time together." She thinks it has become more difficult to tell if Eric has had a bad day,

> because since adolescence he's more often "grumpy" with me and I don't always know if it's for a reason or not. If I have a reason to believe that something happened, I'll try to make him talk about it. But it's not always very successful, since he's not really good at communicating his feelings.

Jessica Holden still tries to show Eric she loves him and cares about him.

> I say things to him, but not as much as I used to. I also am not as affectionate as I used to be, since he's older now, an adolescent male, and I think he needs his distance. I try to cook something that he really likes. He appreciates it. I try not to show him through buying too much, because it always gets out of hand.

When Stanley Gates is 14, Bernice Gates says,

> We both feel we are losing our closeness. We try and figure out why without blaming either of us. His interests are changing. I'm not sure if it is my work or him just maturing that has made the difference. I am having a hard time letting go. His Dad is alive and doesn't give him any time. A sacrifice had to be made in order for us to keep this house. I had to work.

Bernice lists many ways she tries to let Stanley know she loves and cares about him.

> I grab him, hug him, squeeze him, sit next to him. I come right out and tell him. I bring him home things for no apparent reason. We talk. We talk about what love means, how it is expressed. It doesn't mean I let him do what he wants or give him everything he wants. I tell him it means being here for him, especially when he needs me.

The following year, Bernice is still offering nurturance, and Stanley is still resisting.

> We rent videos, watch TV, clean the house together. Stanley might go out to the movies or something with his older brother. He doesn't like to do anything with me anymore unless I'm taking him to the store to buy him something. I still try to hug him and kiss him and joke with him and tease him. He tells me he's too big. It's okay if he kisses me, but not if I kiss him. Having serious affectionate conversations is not okay with him right now. I still bring him things when I'm out at night, like pizza and the big apples he likes.

Bernice even quits her evening job to spend more time with Stanley, but he generally leaves for the recreation center with his friends before she gets home from work in the afternoon and does not usually return home before 9 or 9:30 p.m.

Carl Peters, at 11 years of age, still reaches out for support from his mother, but he often seems unable to benefit from it. When Carl has a nightmare, his mother tries to comfort him, going into his bedroom, sitting with him, asking him about his dream, rubbing his back, and telling him to try to think of pleasant thoughts. When she gets up to go back to her own room, Carl will turn to her in a rage and say, "Is that it? Is that all you're going to do?" In frustration she will ask, "What else do you want me to do?" He'll say, "Forget it! You just don't care! Go back to bed." When Suzanne Peters asks her friends what they do when their children have nightmares, her friends invariably report doing similar things for their children, but with much better results.

Suzanne believes that Carl's after-school arrangement has affected his need for support and even his ability to receive the support she tries to offer. As a result of having to be on his own at a young age and having responsibilities that a child should not have, she believes Carl has become more nervous and anxious about different things. She believes he was left with a feeling of "not being taken care of enough," and therefore now feels more needy of her attention. But this increased dependence on her often makes him angry with her and causes him to be rebellious. He often sees her best efforts to make him feel supported as insignificant gestures, and he sometimes responds with angry outbursts. These outbursts cause her to feel frustrated and may even lead her to reduce her attempts to provide him with support.

Suzanne contrasts Carl with his older brother, who, she believes, is a much more confident kid because he didn't have to deal with being on his own at such a young age. (Although she attributes these problems to Carl's being left alone at an early age, she says the problems first emerged at the time of her separation from her husband, when Carl and his older brother were taken care of after school by a babysitter.)

Toward the end of the study, Suzanne believes Carl would still probably prefer to have her home in the afternoon, but says that even if she were there, he would probably just come in, grab a snack, and leave. "He likes the services a mother can provide but wants to be unfettered. He's like most men."

Peggy Monroe believes Zack might like "the notion of my being here" in the after-school hours, commenting, "He hasn't changed much in that way since he was a little boy." Throughout the study Zack Monroe names his mother as a provider of virtually all the forms of social support we ask about, yet there is often a distance between the type of support he says he would like to receive and the type of support his mother provides. In the first year of the study, Zack names his mother as a provider of all five of the social support resources we ask about. When Zack is asked whether it is true or false that "no one pays much attention to me at home," Zack comments, "Not in the way I need it." Things that make Zack feel worried or sad include bad grades and "my mother being disappointed in me." Zack believes that his mother can usually tell when he is feeling happy and also when he is feeling worried or sad, "but she's usually sad, too." Later in the study, Zack continues to be troubled by his grades. When he is distressed, he says, "usually I try to go to bed and put on some music. If I talk to my mother she'll offer me cocoa, and let me wallow in self-pity." The strong love evident between Zack and his mother, and her provision of social support resources, are not sufficient, somehow, to meet Zack's needs.

THE ADEQUACY OF SOCIAL SUPPORT

> It is pointless to try to assess the quality or quantity of social support experienced by children without considering the nature of the ecological contexts in which the children live, and the fit between the support and the context. (Tietjen, 1989, p. 39)

Children face different sets of challenges during the after-school hours, and the adequacy of their social support networks must be judged in relation to the challenges they face. Eight-year-old Omar Jones, responsible for a 4-year-old brother and a 14-month-old sister in his isolated apartment, faces severe challenges that are not reduced by his mother's anxious telephone calls. Yet telephone calls do provide other children in less tense situations with reassurance, useful advice, and emotional support. Pets can delight, distract, and reassure children who are on their own. They do not help children with other stressful challenges during the after-school hours, such as the need to complete homework and chores without parental prompting.

Siblings often represent conflict as well as support, but the support usually outweighs the conflict. Children help each other enjoy after-school time, they remind each other about obligations such as homework and chores, and they share tasks such as cooking dinner. Even those siblings who quarrel frequently tend to seek out time together, particularly when they are distressed, and to report that their brothers and sisters are support providers. Children who take on responsibility for a younger brother or sister may find their duties frustrating, but they also tend to derive deep satisfactions from their helping role.

Parents who must be absent during the after-school hours are often experienced as emotionally present, while some parents who are physically present are experienced as psychologically absent. Most parents seem able to provide adequate support to their children even though they must be apart during the after-school hours. Some parents are able to communicate by telephone or even to see their children during afternoon visits to the workplace, although others must wait until the work day is over to speak with their children. Mornings, evenings, and weekend time are often used successfully to catch up on the child's daily life and to offer meaningful support. In several families, however, the enforced separation of the after-school hours and the stresses experienced in these hours seem to take a toll on the supportive connections between parents and children. Children who struggle unsuccessfully with the challenges of their after-school arrangements and parents who work particularly long hours at stressful jobs are often not in the best frame of mind to offer and receive support when they are reunited at the end of the work day.

Although families with two parents have the manpower to provide considerable social support to children, no family form has a monopoly on supporting children well. Joint custody families in which the divorced parents had found new spouses or live-in romantic partners could sometimes offer children as many as four concerned adults as support providers. Many single-parent households provided plentiful social support to children, especially when the single parent involved her own siblings and friends as supporters to her children and when she organized and encouraged her children to provide care to each other.

Children also differ in their readiness to respond to offers of social support and in their ability to expand their social networks to meet their own needs. Both boys and girls tend to respond positively to the support providers available to them in the after-school hours, and both boys and girls tend to suffer when their after-school arrangements enforce isolation. Yet when social supports are lacking, girls seem more likely than boys to seek out additional connections with others, often by volunteering their services to responsible adults. Boys are less likely to expand their networks in such ways, and are more likely to forego contact with potential support providers who seem ready and willing to help them. This gender difference is in line with much social support research showing that girls are more likely than boys to seek instrumental help and emotional comfort from others and to be satisfied with the support they receive (Belle, 1989).

It is also possible that boys begin the search for support at a disadvantage. Half of the children in this study lived in single-parent families headed by women. Tietjen (1982) reported that boys in single-parent families have less access to nonrelated adults than do boys in two-parent families or girls in single-mother households. Daughters of single mothers were often included in their mothers' activities with adult friends, and boys from two-parent families often named their fathers' friends as well as the coaches of their sports teams as support providers. Boys in single-mother families had less access to both of these sources of adult companionship. Some of the boys in the present study might have responded more favorably to support offers from male adults who were not readily available to them within the family's social networks.

8

After-School Arrangements and Children's Well-Being

As previous chapters have shown, children's after-school experiences vary in many ways. The presence or absence of adult supervision is only one area in on which after-school arrangements differ, and often this is not the most significant area for children. Adult supervision adds to the safety, direction, comfort, and happiness of many children, but to a few, it is a neutral or even negative aspect of their after-school lives. Unsupervised time is a lonely experience for many children, but a richly supported one for others. To some children, unsupervised time means freedom, while to others it represents valued responsibilities, and to still others it entails onerous restrictions. Unsupervised time leaves one child painfully adrift, liberates the creative energies of another, and feels irrelevant to a third. Some children have unusual inner resources or plentiful social support, while others do not. Children's own appraisals of their after-school settings often seem more powerful than specific "objective" facts about the arrangements in accounting for children's reactions.

Whether supervised or unsupervised, some children find in their after-school arrangements a good match for their own competencies, needs, and desires. Other children with apparently similar arrangements are not well circumstanced or well fitted to make a success of the experience. In many cases, the particular characteristics of a child's after-school arrangements are so deeply intertwined with other important dimensions of their lives that it is difficult to separate the impact of the after-school arrangement from the impact of the on-going life circumstances that helped create the after-school arrangement.

When we first interviewed them, Bonita Moore at 10 years of age and Patricia MacCarthy at 11 had after-school arrangements that were remarkably similar in obvious ways. Both girls spent much of their after-school time without adult supervision, some of this time in the company of their respective older sisters, each of whom was 12 years old. Both girls were also involved in adult-supervised activities during the week, including music lessons or rehearsals (Bonita studied piano, Patricia the trumpet). Bonita practiced gymnastics, and Patricia took a cooking class.

Yet, for all the overt similarity in the way they spent their after-school time, the two girls' experiences could hardly have been more different. To begin with, Bonita helped choose her own after-school arrangement, while Patricia became unsupervised through the force of circumstance. Bonita and her older sister, Barbara, had attended day-care and after-school programs when they were younger, although in the years just prior to the study, their mother worked part time and was home when the girls arrived from school. When Stacey Moore began working full time again (18 months before our first interviews with the family), the girls rebelled against the structured programs they had once attended. The sisters convinced their parents that they could develop their own schedule of activities for after-school time and handle unsupervised time responsibly. In contrast, Patricia and her older sister, Karen, became unsupervised almost accidentally when their father, Bill, took them out of a subsidized day-care program to send them to a 6-week summer camp. After the summer camp was over, the organization that had provided subsidized day care for them could not place them with a babysitter, and Bill could not afford to hire one on his own at market rates.

PATRICIA MACCARTHY'S AFTER-SCHOOL ARRANGEMENTS

Bill MacCarthy, who has sole custody of his daughters, is not at all happy about the arrangements he has for Patricia, and much of his concern centers around the dangers she and her sister face, especially from sexual predators.

> I don't like not having constant supervision available. I do believe that, given the number of "psychos" out there, I'd rather have an adult. I've got two reasonably attractive girls and there's a lot of weirdos out there. And they're friendly, they like talking to people like I do.

Bill's fears are exacerbated because he sees Patricia as overconfident and overeager for a freedom she does not know how to handle. "She wants to be her own boss. She thinks she can do no wrong when she's on her own. She's almost always wrong." Bill sees few redeeming features in his daughter's after-school arrangements: "I think I can say in general that the situation is not beneficial to Patricia. Other than getting time away from me. She wouldn't need much of that anyway, but kids need their own space."

Although Bill cannot be with his daughters after-school and cannot afford to provide alternate adult supervision for them, he attempts to ensure their safety through rules that are meant to govern their behavior. As he stated, "I probably hold the reins a little tighter than most parents." Patricia may only leave the apartment with prior permission or after finishing all of her homework and chores. She can have friends over with her father's prior approval, although this is not often granted. The girls must do their chores first, including cleaning their rooms. "Since they're notoriously lax, they haven't had many people over." Bill says that Patricia's failure to clean her room adequately "has been the biggest point of contention for us." The girls are also responsible, alternately, for cooking dinner and doing the dishes, but for safety's sake they generally wait to begin cooking until Bill has come home.

Patricia cannot visit Bill at work after school. She is allowed to call him on the telephone, but these calls cannot be lengthy or merely social. Bill says Patricia is supposed to limit her calls to emergencies "or if something real important comes up." As Bill sees it, "almost anything will wait for 3 hours." Patricia remembers calling her father recently to ask if she could go to the library, and her father saying, "No, I told you that before." Patricia told him that she had to "study on the Romans," but he repeated his refusal. When Bill is asked about a recent phone call from Patricia, his response is: "I don't remember what it was about. I do remember telling her it was something that could've waited until I got home. Unfortunately that kind of conversation is typical."

Because Patricia spends so much time with her older sister, it is unfortunate that they do not have a better relationship. Patricia says one of the worst things about her after-school arrangement is "having to listen to my sister," and complains that Karen is "bossy" and a "busybody." Patricia says that the only form of social support Karen provides is advice, and that she is also one of the people who makes Patricia feel sad or angry. Patricia gives the lowest possible rating to the time she spends with Karen.

Nor does Patricia have much access in the after-school hours to people outside her family who might be supportive to her. When asked whether there are other people Patricia can call or see during the after-school hours, Bill says that "the only other people I'm friends with aren't home during the day. I know others, but they can't be trusted." He dismisses one particular neighbor as a "flake." Bill appreciates that Patricia would often rather be with her friends after school, but says "I've met some of her friends," and makes disparaging noises. Patricia is thrown on her own resources a great deal.

The physical setting in which she spends most of her after-school time is notably small, cramped, and dismal. Bill is a great science fiction reader, and stacks of books fill the small apartment, blocking one window and occasionally toppling over. Nor does Patricia benefit from these books, as her father does not allow her to read them. Clothes lines stretch across the living room. Within this apartment, Patricia's greatest joy is music, both playing and listening to it. She also reads for pleasure and has begun to write poetry.

Patricia's responses to our questions about her social support network are virtually unique within our study and convey an impression of extreme isolation. The only person she names as providing her with emotional support is a former Big Sister who moved away 3 years prior to the study. When good things happen she doesn't have anyone to tell. "I don't know. I used to have [my Big Sister]. She's the only person I tell anything to." Later she says, "other people don't listen." Patricia is not at all satisfied with the social support she receives from her family and consistently reports less satisfaction with their support than with the support she receives from people outside her family. When Patricia feels worried or sad she says she will "go sit in a corner by myself and [not] talk to anybody." Does she tell people things that happen to her at school? "No. I just don't care about it. Nobody really needs to know. They have their own problems." Bill offers a similar perspective. Asked whether there are certain times of day in which he generally finds out about Patricia's day, he says, simply,

"No." Bill believes that Patricia has special relationships with his sisters, whom she and Karen call to talk with "about report cards, for girl talk, female problems, whatever." Patricia, however, only names her aunts as providers of material goods and services, not as people to whom she can talk about her feelings.

Patricia clearly wishes for more companionship and for more enjoyable activities with friends. When asked whether she has a make-believe friend, Patricia says:

> Sometimes when I'm alone and no one's around I close my eyes on my bed and dream of a friend who has a parent and will do anything with me and the parent will be a chaperone and take us ice skating or something.

Not surprisingly, Patricia's report of her own loneliness is extremely high (two standard deviations above the mean for the sample). However, Patricia's father does not seem to be aware of this problem. In filling out the Child Behavior Checklist, he reports that it is "not true" that Patricia complains of loneliness or is withdrawn. He says it is only "somewhat or sometimes true" that she is unhappy, sad, or depressed. In contrast to his sanguine view about her morale, Bill does report a level of externalizing problems, such as arguing, stubbornness, lying, or cheating, that puts Patricia one standard deviation above the sample mean. He views Patricia as a troublesome child. "I never gave my mother a bit of trouble. Patricia has given me nothing but for the last year." Yet he apparently does not see Patricia's own pain.

There are some positive changes in Patricia's after-school situation in Year 2 of the study, but the problematic aspects continue and some appear to intensify. Most positively, Patricia has been selected for the all-city orchestra, a significant achievement. Her father is proud of and happy for her. "It helps build self-esteem and confidence. She was told she would not be able to do it, she wasn't good enough, and she beat them all." Patricia attends weekly rehearsals for this orchestra, in addition to weekly rehearsals with her school orchestra. In addition, Patricia has begun babysitting a younger boy one afternoon a week. She gives both of these new activities a very positive rating. Yet, at our interview in February, Patricia says that she has been "grounded" since the beginning of the school year, preventing her from visiting or being visited by friends. If she were able to change her after-school arrangements in any way, Patricia would "be able to go out with my friends without my sister bossing me. I'd be able to have fun. I'd feel like me. I'm not used to being stuck in a house."

Her relationship with Karen has not improved. Asked if she is getting closer to her sister because of the unsupervised time they spend together, Patricia says, "No. We don't like each other." The house rules include no fighting between the sisters, "which doesn't work well. We're on each other's bad side all the time." The orchestra rehearsals she now attends are great, "because I feel normal with the trumpet. I get away from my sister." This year, Patricia complains that her father favors and spoils Karen, while Patricia is the one who does all the housework. "My sister never helps. I'm the only one who does the work and my dad says she does it. I do more work around here so I can prove my sister didn't do it." Patricia does not mention her sister as a provider of any positive form of social support, only for exchanges that make Patricia feel sad or angry. Yet when Patricia is asked about times she has felt scared or uncomfortable during the after-school hours, she mentions several occasions, all involving her sister, when Karen did not meet her as expected, or did not come home for hours, or ran away from home.

Patricia's communication with her father is minimal, and conflict between the two is high. When asked if she told her father about her fears about Karen, Patricia responds, "No, he doesn't really listen to me." In her view, "Me and my dad aren't alike, and we don't spend a lot of time together." Patricia sees herself as having no ability to influence family decisions because her father refuses to listen to alternative ideas. "Whatever Dad says goes. He tells us what the rules are." Patricia also admits that she flouts these rules, especially by having friends over to visit despite her father's prohibitions. Her defiance, however, does not give her a feeling of real power within the family. Nor does Patricia feel significantly supported by her father. Although she lists her father and her aunts for several forms of social support in the second year, she continues to rate support from family members more negatively than support from those outside her family.

If she could, Patricia would change a great deal about her after-school arrangements. Visiting friends, attending after-school programs, getting homework help, or going bowling would all be preferred to what she does. Patricia's favorite time of day is "sleeping. I don't have to listen to anybody bossing me around." Once again, her loneliness score is extreme. Once again, her father sees her as having externalizing behavior problems, but misses the loneliness that Patricia conveys so vividly to her interviewer.

Before we returned for our final interviews with Patricia and her father, tragic events took place in the MacCarthy family. Karen ran away from home again, and then moved in with her aunt. Patricia also ran away, was raped, and attempted suicide. Her father's worst nightmare about his daughter was realized. As a result of these events, social service agencies intervened in Patricia's life and arranged for meetings with a therapist and with a therapy group. As if these problems were not enough, Bill had surgery that left him bedridden for an indefinite period. Patricia is now responsible for all of the housework and also must care for her father. These responsibilities have made her late for her beloved orchestra rehearsals and have kept her from doing all of her homework.

Patricia is still having difficulty communicating with her father. "I try to talk to him, the phone rings and ends our conversation. He spends a lot of time on the phone. Sometimes I keep talking, but he gets angry." This year, she lists several friends as people who give her emotional support and help her with her feelings. Yet she still isolates herself when she is worried or sad. "I don't want to be near people. I just don't want to talk to people." When something bad happens she locks herself in her room, turns the stereo to its maximum volume and refuses to talk to anyone. This actually does help her, she says, because "my world totally goes around music. It reflects my mood: classical for happy, hard rock for anger." Once again, Patricia describes frightening levels of loneliness. This year, for the first time, her father also sees such problems, as well as the externalizing problems he had noted in previous years.

BONITA MOORE'S AFTER-SCHOOL ARRANGEMENTS

What Stacey Moore likes best about her daughters' after-school arrangements is that "they take advantage of the options they have." They do have perimeters beyond which they cannot go, but within the geographic area open to them they can do many things they enjoy: ride their bikes, go swimming, visit the library, see friends, go to the store. For Paul Moore, "the passive recipient role of accepting parental entertainment is counterproductive." What he likes best about his daughters' after-school arrangements is "freedom of choice, ruling their own world. They do what they want."

This does not mean that the Moores have no worries when their girls are on their own. These worries are tempered, however, by confidence in the training the girls have received, and by confidence in their maturity. Paul says, "We trust them, trust their judgment. We don't want to make them paranoid, just cautious." Stacey says,

> You have parental fears, like you can't make them paranoid but you have to tell them not to open the door to strangers. I don't worry about carelessness, because I've taught them and they're responsible. I don't worry about them getting into mischief. It's the unknown, someone following them home, not their behavior.

In an ideal world, Stacey would prefer to have "an older teen hanging out with them who's similar to them, who's there if they want to go beyond the perimeters, who could take them places, rather than leaving it to weekends with us."

Paul would "feel better if there was someone here with them. They'd do the same things but have a more immediate adult handy." Unable to find such a person, both parents are quite pleased with the arrangements they do have and believe that their daughters are thriving.

The Moores both work within a short distance of home, and this proximity contributes to their comfort with their daughters' lack of supervision.

> Under the circumstances, I'm only down the street, so they have easy access to me—two blocks. Their Dad works at the corner. If we worked far away I'd be much more uncomfortable. They can drop in, check in.

The character of the neighborhood also increases their confidence. When Stacey was growing up, there were always "siblings and neighbors around who took care of all the kids in the neighborhood," and who were "always watching out." She finds the neighborhood atmosphere her daughters experience today similar to what she herself experienced as a child, the "same sense of community." Paul echoes this thought, praising the "neighborhood network" atmosphere that provides security for his children.

Seeing Bonita and Barbara as having already internalized most of their parents' concerns and values, the Moores do not circumscribe their daughters' behavior very tightly. The girls are free to leave the house, but usually call to tell their mother where they are going and when they will be back. When it comes to having friends visit, there are "no rules if it's friends we know, but they usually ask." Given the girls' busy schedule after school, the Moores make an effort not to require them to do chores beyond simply cleaning up after themselves and helping out when company is coming, for instance. Stacey says, "There are responsibilities I make sure they don't have." About homework, "it's just expected that it's done—unvoiced expectations." Concerning the television,

> they have to monitor themselves. Barbara spends much more time reading. Bonita has to monitor herself and tells me how she'll cut back. Her conscience bothers her because she knows we don't like it.

Cooking is allowed, and the girls sometimes make dinner for the family. When answering the telephone, they avoid telling callers they are home without their parents, saying instead that their mother is busy or at the neighbor's and will be right back. According to Stacey, this rule is one the girls heard somewhere and adopted themselves, not a rule imposed by either parent. As this example suggests, the girls' rules change over time, often because of suggestions from Bonita and Barbara. Paul says,

> As they grow older they request changes in the rules based on their increased levels of responsibility and maturity. Sometimes rules just stop being enforced because they are not actual anymore.

Rules are "not a big deal" in the Moore household, and neither is punishment. "We're not into punishment. We are into limit setting. Praise is easier to give."

Although the Moores do not restrict their daughters with many rules, the girls take seriously the rules they do have. Stacey tells about one time when she went to meet the girls after an evening activity. When she arrived she found they had already left, so she returned home. The girls reminded her that she had told them always to walk on a particular street when traveling between this activity and their house. They had done so, but their mother, having forgotten the rule, had chosen another route.

Bonita and her sister can call and even visit both parents with ease after school. Both parents emphasize that the girls can call anytime, and Paul says, "They have total access to both of us. They know that even if we're in a meeting, they can tell whoever answers the phone it is important and they'll get us." Bonita believes that she and her sister "can call whenever we want. If they are in a meeting, their children come first."

Bonita says her parents each call her every day to ask about her day. Stacey likes to call, "just to see how their day was, how they felt, what they were doing." Being able to have her daughters visit her at work was something Stacey arranged when she first took her job. "When I was hired I specifically asked and it was never a problem." After she had been on the job for some time she returned from an evening meeting to find that there had been a power failure when Bonita was home by herself. She had lit candles in each of the rooms, but Stacey could tell she had been scared. As a result of this incident, Stacey asked that evening meetings at work start earlier and end earlier, "and if they're not done by 8 p.m. it's understood that I leave." Stacey can also bring work home if she wants to spend more time with the girls. Stacey has always worked for women's organizations, and she believes such organizations are supportive of women with children. "They give you no flack. As long as you do your job, you're okay."

Bonita and Barbara are often together in the after-school hours, and, happily, their relationship is a mutually supportive one. Over the course of the study, Bonita always names Barbara as providing most or all of the support resources we ask about and rates the time she spends with her quite highly. Barbara typically names Bonita as providing several forms of support and rates positively the time they spend together. Barbara is someone Bonita often talks with when she is worried or sad about something, and Bonita believes that Barbara can sometimes tell her things she can not tell their parents. Of course, there are arguments and conflicts between the girls, "almost classic stuff," according to their mother. "You have on my sweater!" "Well, you have on my pants!" But Stacey believes the girls are "very close. They have a special bond. They really love each other. They like each other."

Beyond her immediate family, Bonita has access to many of her friends and neighbors in the after-school hours. Stacey feels very strongly that the girls should have as many friends come to visit as they want. "People are in and out of the house. I'll come home from work and see the girls' friends lying on the couch. I love it." According to Paul, the neighborhood is a friendly one. "People are out on their stoops or in their yards, and they just stop and chat."

Supportive family members are available to Bonita during much of the day. Stacey says she is a morning person, and the time she spends most with the girls is in the morning. She is always up before them so she can greet them when they come down or even kiss them awake.

> Sometimes they're just on my bed in the morning ready to have a long, serious conversation. That's important time for us, getting the day going, cooling out any stress, getting them ready. Their days are hectic enough so they have to start with as much security as possible before they leave.

Paul comes to the fore in the evening, chauffering the girls to lessons or out to eat and helping with homework. Bonita says that her favorite time of the day is evening. "Most of my family is home and we get a movie to watch."

When problems arise during the after-school hours, Bonita can talk about them later with family members and friends and these discussions make her feel better. Toward the end of the study, Bonita describes an occasion when one of the children at the day-care center where she works fell and hit her head. Bonita was scared about what was going to happen to the child. "I didn't know how badly hurt she was. My boss was on the phone, in the office. I was the only one with the kids." When Bonita got home she started talking about it, "to everyone in my family," and "it calmed me down." She also told her friends at school.

> Everyday when we first get together we find out what the others did after school the day before, what they did in the evening, even what they had for dinner. It's part of our routine.

For Bonita, experiences of all sorts are discussed with others, and these discussions are helpful.

Bonita is generally pleased with her after-school arrangements:

> It's neat because you can think or have friends over. You don't have to worry about parents saying, "Be quiet," or "Turn down that music." I can go outside and play in the park across the street—so my parents can see me through the window when they get home.

What Bonita does not like about her after-school arrangements is, "If I get bored and I feel like there's nobody to play with." When this happens she usually watches some television, plays games, or invites a friend over. "Sometimes my older sister is home with me, but she plays volleyball after school a lot." If she could change her after-school arrangement in any way, Bonita would still like to be at home, but would like more company. Stacey is aware that Bonita would like to spend more time with friends from school, and explains that these arrangements are not made easily because the school is not nearby.

> Other than that she likes the busy afternoons with her sister and the afternoon she knows her sister's not around. I thought I'd see her all the time at my work, but she likes that time for herself.

Stacey credits her daughters with creating a superior after-school arrangement to the one she had originally intended for them. "The poor kids would probably still be in an after-school program bored to death. They've gained more than they would have by going in the direction I would have sent them in."

Later she notes,

> I had a lot of resistance a few years ago to them having so much decision-making power around their free time but it worked out well for them. I have confidence in their ability to work out a schedule of activities that I won't disapprove of. There's nothing worse than working and worrying about your children. It's almost impossible to do both, and I haven't had to worry in a long time. I can't think of anything I don't like about the after-school arrangement. It's as close as you could get to a perfect situation.

Paul says he "delights" in his daughters' "growth and increased confidence." Their arrangements combine independence ("They're out in the world") and safety ("They've lived in this neighborhood all their lives and have confidence in it.")

POINTS OF COMPARISON

Although Patricia MacCarthy and Bonita Moore could properly be characterized as girls who divide their after-school time between adult-supervised activities, time with an older sister, and time on their own, the differences between the arrangements of the two girls are more striking than the similarities. To begin with, Bonita and her older sister chose to be unsupervised after school and they continue to shape their after-school arrangements. (When asked in one interview what she liked least about her after-school arrangements, Bonita's sister, Barbara, answered, "I liked everything I did 'cause I chose it.") Patricia MacCarthy, in contrast, has never had much say about what she does in the after-school hours. Patricia's unsupervised time is spent in a confined space with a very limited cast of characters, while Bonita has an entire neighborhood open for her exploration and access to many friendly adults and children. Bonita can easily visit her parents at work or speak with them on the telephone, and they welcome these contacts. Patricia cannot visit her father at work and her telephone calls are discouraged. Patricia is heavily burdened with housework and chores and finds little time in the after-school period to do things she enjoys. Bonita has few household responsibilities and is encouraged to pursue her own interests during the after-school hours. Both girls spend after-school time with their older sisters, yet Patricia's sister seems only to heighten her distress, while Bonita's sister functions as an important support provider.

The Moores illustrate the authoritative parenting style, in which parents retain ultimate authority within the family but consider the views of their children in making decisions. Bill MacCarthy functions as an authoritarian parent, making decisions for his children without taking into consideration their preferences and opinions. In line with previous research on parenting style and children who are unsupervised after school (L. Steinberg, 1986), the Moore's authoritative parenting, not Bill MacCarthy's authoritarian parenting, is associated with benign outcomes.

The Moores make a point of asking about Bonita's day, listening to her when she wants to talk, and helping her prepare for and respond to stressful episodes in her life. Bill MacCarthy tends to repress Patricia's attempts at communication and makes little effort to inform himself about her day-to-day experiences. Perhaps in response to these very different parenting styles, Bonita tends to discuss her life with family members and friends, seeking out their support when she is stressed, and experiencing this support as calming and reassuring, while Patricia isolates herself and rarely shares her experiences with others.

The Moore family has many resources that help to make a desirable after-school arrangement possible for their daughters. In contrast to the MacCarthy family they have two parents to share the burdens of running a household and to provide support to the children. In addition, the Moores both have master's degrees, while Bill MacCarthy has only a high school diploma. Higher education allows the Moores to earn higher salaries, which gives them more choice of neighborhood and housing. They are attached to their neighborhood and have faith in their neighbors. They have been able to choose jobs very close to their home and to insist on flexibility at work to respond to their children's needs. Bill MacCarthy, in contrast, must accept the restrictions on family involvement that come with his job. His negative view of his neighborhood and his neighbors may well be associated with his inability to afford housing elsewhere.

Stacey Moore is African American, while Bill MacCarthy is White, and it may be that the Moore family's strong sense of connection to neighbors and family friends reflects a cultural heritage that emphasizes interdependence within and between families.

PARENTAL GOALS AND VALUES

Although some after-school arrangements seem conspicuously successful and others less so, it is also worthwhile to examine the definition of what constitutes a successful after-school arrangement. Parental goals for children differ, and parents have different expectations for the challenges their children will face in the future and for the skills and personality attributes that will be most essential in meeting these challenges.

Tietjen (1989) argued that notions of successful adaptation vary with the demands made on individuals by their cultures. In highly individualistic societies in which adult success is strongly linked to academic achievement, we appropriately measure competence by assessing school competence, the ability to interact effectively with peers, and self-esteem. In cultures that instead stress integration and interdependence within the group, central aspects of competence would probably include "the ability to perform tasks that contribute to the welfare of the community; the ability to interact effectively with people of all ages; a sensitivity to the needs of others; and the ability to subordinate one's own needs to those of the community" (Tietjen, 1989, p. 43).

Western psychologies, following the dominant value systems of Western societies, have typically stressed the development of the autonomous individual, although women, many minority groups, and non-Western societies have generally been more concerned with issues of relatedness (Guisinger & Blatt, 1994). Some critics suggest that emphasizing the values of autonomy, independence, and individual achievement, to the exclusion of relational concerns, accounts for much of the alienation experienced within the Western world (Guisinger & Blatt, 1994).

In this study, several families evidenced a strongly interdependent view of family life and encouraged mutual support between siblings and among members of the extended family. Emilie Perry's mother died when she was 5 years old, and Emilie's aunt reared her and her five brothers and sisters. Perhaps with this important lesson in mind Emilie now encourages her own daughter, Jasmin, to turn readily to her aunts and godmother for social support. According to Jasmin, Emilie has also told her children that they must stay together throughout life, because if she is not there, they will always be there for each other. Similarly, Eleanor Townsend has spoken to her older son about the necessity and value of his sibling caretaking, explaining to him "that we were a family, and that was the only way we could make it together." George and Michael spend much of their after-school time "within eye's reach" of each other, and George willingly sacrifices time he might spend on sports to be at home with his younger brother.

Families noteworthy for their emphasis on interdependence and mutuality were often African-American families. Although several of these families were among the poorest in the study, they were remarkably rich in love and connection. Sibling caretaking was prevalent, and sibling relationships were strong. Previous research has found that sibling caretaking is especially frequent among African Americans (Cutler et al., 1995), and B. Williams (1992) has argued that if we assessed family strength using sibling ties rather than marital ties, Blacks would be seen as having stronger families than Whites.

Jocelyn Williams is also African American, and she does not emphasize interdependence for her children. While Emilie Perry reflects back on the aunt who took over mothering duties for her family, Jocelyn remembers the many times her brother left her alone after school when she was assigned to his care, believing that she could take care of herself. Jocelyn's mission is to prove herself self-reliant and to ensure that her daughter and her son can function effectively on their own without help from anyone. She trains her children to handle time on their own responsibly and even to provide their own emotional support and reassurance in times of stress. She worries about coddling the children by staying home from work with them when they are sick, and she does not encourage family togetherness. Jocelyn's own life has taught her that an individual must be able to take care of him or herself, because there may well be no one else around to take care of her.

In the Somers family, all of the family members we interviewed placed a particularly high value on the pursuit of excellence, commitment to tasks that had been undertaken, and mastery of athletic, academic, and musical skills. Peter Somers models this commitment to excellence and to athletic competence by playing basketball after work every day, sometimes returning home in the evening after the children have gone to bed. Micah would like to spend more time with his father, but shares his father's dedication to training and his love of sports. According to Peter, "time is precious," and he is pleased that his children are learning to use it wisely. Peter believes that "achievement is important" to Micah. "He likes excelling." Laura Peters believes that her children's after-school activities give them "a sense of direction, purpose, the meaning of commitment. They have to get themselves to practice, to be at meetings. They have to be responsible." She is pleased that her children stick with things they have begun, that they persevere. They are also learning a great array of skills that they can build on long into adulthood. Although she can not be sure they will make the time for these things when they grow up, she knows many adults who say, "I wish my mother had made me stick with piano," and she does not want her children to have those regrets. Micah Somers believes that because of what he does after school he is getting better "in everything—piano, sports, tap dancing." He has had to quit his basketball team because of the demands of his soccer team, "but usually I don't quit anything. I like to stick with things even if they're hard." He shares his parents' appreciation for excellence, commitment to what he has begun, and skill learning.

Families, of course, often embody multiple values. The Townsend family values academic and athletic success as well as interdependence, and George is a successful athlete and student. The Somers family values closeness between the children, and Micah Somers enjoys a mutually supportive relationship with his sister. Yet families do differ in the strength of their attachment to different value systems. One family might see "success" in an after-school arrangement that does not seem successful at all to another family.

RESOURCES

Although Micah Somers and his sister engage in a dizzying round of lessons and activities after school, Peter Somers says that his children's after-school arrangements are "very doable, not overwhelming." He credits "having two cars, a location convenient to public transportation, a neighborhood where people get together," and a two-parent family. "You may have noticed that in [this community] an intact family is in a minority. Having two parents is helpful." As discussed earlier in this chapter, the Moores also have many resources, including flexible nearby jobs and friendly neighbors, that help them provide a positive after-school experience for their daughters.

In contrast to the experiences of the Moores and the Somers family, many parents in this study are unable to provide for their children the kinds of after-school experiences they desire. Low-income parents often wish they could afford the gymnastics classes, dancing lessons, or karate classes their children request, or that they could provide transportation so that their children could take advantage of educational opportunities, such as a reading program at a nearby university. Although values motivate parents in particular directions, parents are not always able to act on the values they hold.

SETTINGS

Micah Somers' location on a dead-end street near to his school and a large park would be the envy of many children and parents in the study. Julie Samuels lives on a street with heavy and dangerous traffic, and perhaps because of this there are virtually no other children who live nearby and who can be visited without parental assistance. Gregory Polansky finds nothing of interest within walking distance of his house, and Stanley Gates cannot leave his own street because of the danger of crime in his neighborhood. The particular settings in which children spend after-school hours can have considerable power in shaping the nature of their after-school time.

VULNERABILITY AND RESILIENCE

In studying why some children cope well with challenging experiences and others are less successful, researchers have noted that resilient children are both sociable and autonomous. They can provide their own structure when necessary, and they can also ask for support when they need it (Werner, 1990). This characterization of resilient children is also an excellent description of the children in this study who coped well with challenging after-school experiences. Such children successfully created structure in otherwise unstructured time, and they also maintained relationships with supportive adults and children, including those who were not physically present with them in the after-school period.

Children who coped successfully with difficult after-school arrangements often exhibited a strong identification with one or both parents.

They shared the values their parents espoused and they endorsed the rules and guidelines their parents laid down for after-school time. Dominique Nelson, who does her own schoolwork and considerable housework while caring for her younger sister after-school, says she likes the fact that her mother works. "I feel almost like my mother. I have to babysit—that's fun. I have to take care of stuff. I have to be responsible." Ruby Nelson says she and Dominique are "more like a team than mother and daughter." Both describe a very close, affectionate, and mutually appreciative relationship that appears strengthened, if anything, by Ruby's absences during after-school hours.

Dominique's behavior and attitudes are reminiscent of the "caring-competent" children, most of them girls, whom Hetherington (1989) discovered when she studied children's adjustment to parental divorce. These children were high in self-esteem, popular with both peers and teachers, low in behavior problems, and successful academically. They were also particularly high in helping and sharing behavior. Caring-competent girls had employed single-parent mothers who encouraged their mature independent behavior. The mothers were usually warm and supportive but not always available. Caring-competent girls were also distinctive in that they had assumed responsibility for the care of siblings or other family members at a young age.

Hetherington's findings on caring-competent children are in line with other studies that implicate "required helpfulness" as a protective factor for children in times of stress (Elder, 1974; Werner & Smith, 1982). Medrich et al. (1982) reported a similar phenomenon. "Our data showed that children with important roles to play at home, though they did not necessarily like their jobs, did have higher self-esteem" (p. 246).

GENDER

In this study, girls seemed to have several advantages when confronting unsupervised and unstructured after-school time. Girls seemed to seek out more social support and to be more satisfied with the social support they received. Girls seemed more easily to form strong identifications with their parents, particularly in comparison to boys in single-mother households. Previous research also suggests that boys may experience more difficulty connecting with parents when their mothers are employed and therefore less available to them (Richards & Duckett, 1991). Parents may seek out boys less often than girls, assuming that boys do not need as much parental contact and supervision as do girls. Yet boys may actually need more structure (Richards & Duckett, 1991). In divorced families, Hetherington, Cox, and Cox (1982) found that structure and control appeared more important in fostering resilience in boys, whereas nurturance and responsibility were more important for girls.

CONCLUSION

Successful coping with challenging after-school arrangements reflects qualities of the child, the parent–child relationship, and the settings in which the child spends after-school time. Understanding adaptation requires attention to all of these factors and to their interplay.

9

Implications

The question for us as we watch the procession of people move each morning from private house to public world is not, Who can we blame? We have to ask ourselves here and now, What are we as a nation, a culture, a society going to do about the children who are being left behind?

—Martin (1992, p. 4)

The after-school hours present employed parents and their children with dilemmas that are not easy to resolve. By the age of 10 or 11 or even before, many children are spending some unsupervised time before their parents return for the day from work. Some children do seem ready for the considerable independence and responsibility they experience after school. They and their parents should not be stigmatized because the children are unsupervised after school. Yet, other children are clearly unready for the challenges they face during the after-school hours when adults are not with them.

PUBLIC POLICY ISSUES

Many of the children in the present study would benefit from after-school programs that are not currently available to them, either because their parents cannot afford the programs, they have no transportation to or from the programs, or appropriate programs simply do not exist where they are.

Because this study was conducted in a metropolitan area unusually well served by after-school programs and by public transportation, the unmet needs in many other parts of the country are almost certainly greater. When parents cannot resolve their after-school dilemmas alone, it is time for the larger society to find ways to assist them and their children. Additional funding is essential to create more after-school programming, to subsidize access to this programming for children who would not otherwise benefit from it, and to subsidize transportation to and from after-school activities for children who need this assistance.

In this study, several children were removed from after-school programs because they encountered repeated violence from other children, harsh punishments or inattention from after-school teachers, intolerable levels of noise, or a dearth of engaging activities. These are not trivial concerns. To bring the quality of such programs in line with the best after-school programs children and parents described may well require finding alternate physical settings, hiring more after-school teachers, improving the training and supervision of teachers, and seriously increasing the funding available to make these improvements possible.

Yet even the provision of high-quality after-school programs will fail to solve the problems of families in which parents have to work more than one full-time job, and children are unsupervised well into the evening, at night, or during weekend hours. One response to such families would be to revive the Lanham Act and re-open government-funded child-care centers that operate around the clock, as was done for the children of some women factory workers during World War II. An alternative strategy is to put more money in the hands of parents who have low-wage jobs so that one full-time job is sufficient for the economic needs of the family. Wages for many Americans have declined substantially since the 1970s in inflation-adjusted dollars. As Jocelyn Williams says, life is tougher now, and many U. S. parents are working longer hours simply to hold onto their houses or apartments and to make ends meet. Increases in the minimum wage and enhancements in the Earned Income Tax Credit, which allows low-wage parents to keep more of their income, would do a great deal to help children, by helping their parents forego the second job or lengthy overtime hours that keep them away from home.

Putting more money in the hands of low-income parents may also allow them to resolve their after-school dilemmas in other ways, by making it possible to afford babysitters, after-school activities, or transportation to and from activities. Families' problems are often idiosyncratic, and measures that increase a family's ability to resolve its own problems in its own way offer the most promise. More disposable income will help low-income families make the decisions that work best for them.

It may also be timely to reconsider the 6-hour school day and the annual school calendar, with its lengthy summer vacation. We are no longer primarily an agricultural nation, in which children's labor is needed on the farm, yet the school calendar continues to reflect its origins in our now remote past. Today, most parents work outside the home, and do so for longer than 6 hours each day. Nor are there pressing pedagogical arguments for retaining the 6-hour school day or the current school calendar. Many other industrialized nations school children for more days each year or more hours per day or both. Lengthening the school day or the school year would probably have educational advantages for children's learning, as well as helping to close the gap between the time at which children leave school and the time at which their employed parents arrive home to join them.

Similarly, we should rethink the frequency of early release days and other interruptions to the regular school week. Even parents who have arranged regular after-school care for their children are often unable to provide adult supervision when schools close in the middle of the day. Although early release days allow teachers to do important work, it should be possible to continue such work while also providing substitute care for children.

Employers should be challenged to find ways to allow employees who are parents to care for their children properly. Parents who can make and receive telephone calls at work, bring children to the workplace on occasion, and take time off from work to be with their children at home will do a better job of parenting and may actually be more productive at work as their anxiety about their children's safety decreases. Businesses might also find that the favorable publicity they could generate for relatively inexpensive "family-friendly" policies would make such measures cost effective. Although not all work settings can accommodate parents in every way, most work settings probably could do more for parents and children if they saw this as a priority. Modern technology, including pagers and cellular telephones, can allow parents to receive messages from their children even if they are away from traditional telephones, for instance.

Parents report the least flexibility at work when they have limited education and work for low wages. Employers may believe that such employees have few employment alternatives, and may therefore make little attempt to support such employees in their parental responsibilities. Government action, building on legislation such as the Family and Medical Leave Act, may be necessary if employers do not act on their own to aid employees in fulfilling their obligations as parents.

As children enter early adolescence, they often become impatient with the sort of after-school programs they had enjoyed in the past and wish for more freedom in the after-school hours. These wishes appear reasonable when one reflects on the situations in which children of this age generally find themselves when their parents are at home to supervise them. In safe neighborhoods, at least, 10- or 11-year-old children are often at a considerable distance from their parents, exploring their communities, visiting friends, or playing in parks and fields. They may be with other children or alone. They may spend time close to adults or at some distance from them. They have the flexibility to experience solitude or to engage with others. In contrast, the logistics of traditional after-school programs generally demand that children remain within the visual field of responsible adults and in space shared with many other children. Alternative after-school arrangements that offer children more freedom while still providing some monitoring and some support would probably engage many early adolescents who now agitate for an end to adult supervision altogether.

Discussion of children's after-school experiences often has the unfortunate effect of treating school-age children as problems. This stance ignores the very real resources that these same children can provide. Several of the children in this study are already serious household workers and sibling caretakers. Others help teachers, librarians, and school counselors, and work at day-care centers or as babysitters or in a parent's store. This work contributes needed resources to children's families, schools, and communities, and it is also often deeply gratifying to the child workers. We could do much more to tap the nurturant and altruistic potential of children in the after-school hours by focusing on children as potential workers and helpers, rather than simply as individuals in need of assistance.

Although children bear the brunt of unsatisfactory after-school arrangements, parents also have after-school problems. Many live with considerable anxiety about their children's welfare. Many cope with the stigma of allowing children to be unsupervised. This stigma, in turn, may make it more difficult to protect children who are unsupervised because parents may fear letting even potential support figures know of the child's after-school situation.

This study converges with others in showing that many parents, especially mothers, tailor their work lives to the vagaries of the school calendar and the 6-hour school day. Although some parents would choose to spend more time with their children no matter what options were available for the children's after-school care, others regret the professional and economic sacrifices they must make to assure their children's well-being in the after-school hours. The implications of such underemployment for family finances, for the morale of working parents, and for the national economy deserve serious consideration.

ISSUES FOR PARENTS

It would be convenient if there were a specific age at which children always became ready for unsupervised time, or if there were a limited number of variables that could infallibly predict any given child's readiness. Life is more complicated, however. In considering what after-school arrangements to make for children, parents need to consider the child's particular strengths and vulnerabilities as well as the hazards and supports associated with the settings in which the child might spend after-school time. Parental goals and values are also highly personal and will vary from family to family.

Unsupervised time often presents stressful challenges to children. Children are likely to meet these challenges most successfully when they are able both to function independently and to sustain supportive relationships with others. Children who cannot regulate their own behavior in the absence of adults and those who have difficulty eliciting or accepting social support are unlikely to do well in unsupervised settings, no matter how intelligent and sensitive they are. Children also fare best when their parents convey sustained interest in their well-being and when communication between parents and children is strong. Authoritative parenting, in which parents attend to the children's wishes and concerns while retaining ultimate authority in the family, seems especially advantageous for children coping with after-school time on their own.

Talking with children about their after-school experiences is an excellent way for parents to increase their understanding of the strengths and vulnerabilities their children bring to after-school arrangements as well as the hazards and supports their children encounter in different settings. Over half the mothers in this study said that simply being in the study, being asked questions about their children's after-school experiences, changed their thinking about the issue in some way. Many said it stimulated more conversations with the children about their lives after school. In some cases, these conversations made parents aware of problems they had not known about before or revealed to parents the full extent of a problem they had thought was minor. Children may not volunteer information about their loneliness or anxiety during the after-school hours, wishing to save their parents worry. Asking children explicitly about their experiences and feelings can reassure children that their parents do want to know about their problems and can encourage children to give their parents a fuller understanding of their day-to-day experiences after school. Parents can then use this richer information to make more informed decisions for their children.

Talking to children about their after-school experiences is also crucial because this is the only way that parents can learn how children subjectively understand and make sense of their after-school experience. It may seem to a parent that a child's situation is perfectly safe, but the child may be hearing burglars at the door or seeing monsters under the bed. A parent may intend that her absence in the afternoon conveys to her child her trust and respect for his judgment. The child, however, may feel inexplicably abandoned. Only in talking seriously with children can we learn how they view the world and how their after-school situations look to them.

Research on children's after-school experiences can continue to help parents by alerting them to risk and support factors they may have overlooked and by exploring the processes by which children's after-school arrangements may have an impact on their emotional and behavioral well-being.

Parents who are dissatisfied with the after-school possibilities for their children may wish to seek out other parents with similar concerns and then present these concerns to political leaders, school personnel, community groups, business groups, religious organizations, and others who could contribute to real solutions. The highly individualistic nature of U. S. society encourages parents to regard their childrearing dilemmas as personal. Yet when millions of other families face identical or related dilemmas, it makes more sense to work for community-based or society-based solutions.

RESEARCH ISSUES

Because there is often no clear demarcation between self-care and supervised time, after-school arrangements can more usefully be understood as existing along a continuum of care, from most to least supervised (Todd, Albrecht, & Coleman, 1990). Children's experiences suggest several dimensions along which their relationships with adults in their after-school settings could be evaluated. Given that an adult is present, does this adult acknowledge responsibility for the child? Is the adult available to the child only in emergencies or also during normal times without emergencies? Does the adult actively monitor the child's behavior, limiting potentially dangerous activities? Does the adult structure the child's use of time, providing activities and materials? Is the adult emotionally supportive? Is the adult accessible to the child on the child's own terms? The variable we have called *supervision* can be disaggregated in this way to reveal various forms of supervision, including supervision as protection from external dangers and temptations, supervision as stimulation to provide an optimal use of leisure time, and supervision as emotional support.

Previous research has pointed to distal supervision by parents, parenting style, and the parent–child relationship as important to the well-being of self-care children (Galambos & Maggs, 1991b; L. Steinberg, 1986). Other work suggests that the presence of siblings in the after-school setting is crucial (Berman et al., 1992; Long & Long, 1982). Future research can profitably investigate the entire cast of characters present with the child during the after-school period or accessible by visit or telephone, as well as the ongoing relationships the child maintains with parents, siblings, friends, and extended family. The simple presence of an individual should not be taken to constitute positive support from that individual. Investigators should be open to the possibility that the involvement of particular people may have negative, rather than positive, implications for children.

For many children, self-care is accompanied by serious responsibilities for younger siblings and for household work. Future studies of after-school arrangements should assess the extent of such responsibilities and their impact on children's well-being. Although sibling caretaking has received some attention, it is most often the younger sibling whose well-being is studied. We should also expect consequences for children charged with nurturing and caring for others.

With sibling caretaking, as with other aspects of after-school arrangements, we should also try to capture more than simply the objective features of the arrangement. Children often react differently to objectively similar arrangements because of the ways they understand and make sense of the arrangements. In studying sibling caretaking, for instance, researchers should ask how children understand their responsibilities: as an expression of parental trust and respect?, as part of an interdependent and loving family system?, or as the result of parental irresponsibility or neglect? Answers to such questions will probably explain more of the variance in the outcomes of family responsibilities than will objective measures such as the number of caretaking hours per week or the number of household chores that parents require. An additional step, of course, is to investigate the sources of children's different ways of understanding after-school responsibilities.

Most research on after-school arrangements has focused on behavioral, academic, and emotional adjustment as outcome variables. An experience such as caring for a younger sibling may well have an impact on such variables, but it may also teach useful caretaking skills, promote nurturance as a value, increase sensitivity to others, and promote the ability to put the needs of others ahead of one's own needs. In addition, the experience of a sibling caretaking relationship may well deepen the affection siblings feel for each other or their sense of the importance of the sibling relationship in their lives. Future research should expand the range of assessments to include attention to such relational outcomes.

After-school arrangements differ in the array of settings and activities that are accessible to children. Future research should investigate children's geographic reach during the after-school hours (e.g., confined to apartment or street vs. able to travel greater distances and visit locations such as parks, friends' houses, etc.) as well as the number and variety of activities available to children at these settings. Rosenthal and Vandell (1996) found that favorable staff–child interactions are more frequent in after-school programs with a greater number of different activities available to children. Children's self-care arrangements may vary even more dramatically than their supervised arrangements in the range of opportunities available to children and in the significance to children of this range of options.

The quality of after-school programs is a pressing topic for further investigation because children's experiences vary enormously from one program to another. Aspects of after-school programs that can be regulated, such as the training of after-school teachers, the teacher to child ratio, and the size and facilities of the physical space the program inhabits should receive first priority (Rosenthal & Vandell, 1996). It is also important to examine how various dimensions of after-school programs serve different populations of children. Older children have different needs than younger ones, and children's needs may well also differ by gender, social class, and personality variables.

This study converges with cross-sectional studies in finding that older children are more likely than younger ones to experience self-care, but the longitudinal nature of the present study also reveals that children sometimes move "backwards" from self-care to adult supervision. Future research could test the proposition that adult supervision for former self-care children is often less rigorous than for those who have never been without adult supervision, particularly when such supervision comes about almost accidentally when parents lose a job or an adult relative moves into the household. In contrast, adult supervision may be especially intense when children reenter supervision in response to a personal or family crisis.

In this study members of the same family often described children's after-school arrangements in discrepant ways. As with other elements of family life, children's after-school arrangements exist in the eyes of the beholders, and different family members may understand the child's arrangements in very different ways. Future research could focus on such discrepancies and attempt to illuminate the origins of different understandings within the family as well as the impact of these divergent views. Do discrepant understandings reduce tension between family members who might otherwise be in conflict over the child's use of after-school time? Do seriously discrepant understandings between husbands and wives signal underlying difficulties in the marriage and a generalized failure of communication?

Children are often powerful forces in modifying their own after-school arrangements and future research should focus more on the active roles children take in changing their own arrangements. Some children seek out adult supervision by volunteering to work with responsible adults. Others evade contact with tutors, babysitters, their own parents, and other available adults. Some children closely abide by parental rules, whereas others bend or flout these rules. Several parents in the study decided against hiring a babysitter because they believed their children would not obey such a person or decided against an after-school program because they believed their children would be miserable at the program or would not attend. Children also lobby their parents to enroll them in particular activities or after-school programs or to remove them from programs and allow for more unsupervised time in the afternoon. Children's personalities and their predilections for certain kinds of after-school arrangements may help to bring about those after-school arrangements, just as after-school arrangements may bring about changes in children's emotional and behavioral adjustment.

Children's after-school experiences seem in some ways to be gendered (Crouter & McHale, 1993), with girls having certain advantages when they confront the challenge of after-school time. Boys seem less likely to mobilize social support, less likely to identify with a parent in undertaking sibling caretaking or household work, and less likely to create satisfying structure in the after-school hours when adults are not available to do so for them. This study is thus more in accord with the body of research on gender differences in children's reactions to maternal employment, which has tended to find greater vulnerability among males, than it is with research on children's adjustment to unsupervised after-school time, which generally finds greater risks for girls. Future research should certainly attend to the ways in which after-school experiences may differ for boys and for girls, and should investigate gender differences in children's ways of coping with stressful after-school experiences.

Increased understanding of the implications of children's after-school arrangements will come as we attend more closely to children's diverse experiences during the after-school hours and continue to develop a more differentiated view of after-school arrangements for children.

Appendix: Demographic Characteristics of the Focus Children at the Start of the Study

Note: Abbreviations are as follows:

Sex: F = female, M = male
Household Structure: 1P = single-parent, 2P = two-parent, JC = joint custody
Household Income:
0 = less than $10,000, 1 = between $10,000 and $20,000, 2 = between $20,000 and $30,000, 3 = between $30,000 and $40,000, 4 = between $40,000 and $50,000, 5 = over $50,000
Mother's Education: 1 = less than high school diploma,
2 = high school diploma or equivalent, 3 = some college, 4 = college degree, 5 = some post-graduate education, 6 = post-graduate degree
Race/Ethnicity: A = Asian American, B = Black, H = Hispanic, W = White
Note that Patricia MacCarthy lives with her single-parent father.

Name	Sex	Age	Household Structure	Household Income	Mother's Education	Race/ Eth.
Banducci, Gabrielle	F	11	1P	2	4	W
Berger, Marguerite	F	9	1P	1	3	B
Castillo, Irene	F	7	1P	1	3	H
Chen, Meiguei	F	7	2P	0	4	A
Colby, Alana	F	10	2P	4	6	W
Cole, Brian	M	9	JC	2	3	W
Delaney, Evan	M	10	JC	5	6	W
Edwards, Cynthia	F	8	1P	2	5	W
Ferraro, Carmen	F	12	1P	1	6	W
Foster, Tori	F	11	1P	2	4	W
Gates, Stanley	M	12	1P	1	3	B
Hardy, Diana	F	10	1P	0	3	W
Hayes, Yvonne	F	7	1P	2	4	W

Name	Sex	Age	Household Structure	Household Income	Mother's Education	Race/ Eth.
Henderson, Louisa	F	12	2P	5	6	W
Holden, Eric	M	12	1P	2	3	W
Jackson, Martha	F	9	1P	2	4	B
Jones, Omar	M	8	2P	1	2	B
Kelley, Michelle	F	9	2P	4	5	W
Kelliher, Mary Ellen	F	8	1P	0	1	W
King, Tasha	F	11	1P	2	4	B
Latimore, Frank	M	10	1P	1	1	B
Lavelle, Nick	M	10	1P	1	3	W
Lawrence, Melissa	F	11	1P	1	4	W
Lehman, Jason	M	8	JC	1	3	W
Linden, Derek	M	7	1P	4	4	W
Lynch, Alex	M	10	2P	5	6	W
MacCarthy, Patricia	F	11	1P	3	2	W
Martell, Bertha	F	7	2P	5	6	W
Monroe, Zack	M	11	1P	2	5	W
Moore, Bonita	F	10	2P	5	6	B
Myers, Rebecca	F	9	2P	2	4	W
Nelson, Dominique	F	10	1P	1	2	B
Perry, Jasmin	F	10	1P	1	2	B
Peters, Carl	M	11	1P	2	6	W
Polansky, Gregory	M	11	2P	5	4	W
Robinson, Shavonne	F	8	2P	2	3	B
Rose, Jennifer	F	7	JC	2	3	W
Samuels, Julie	F	7	1P	2	6	W
Schapiro, Benjamin	M	9	2P	5	4	W
Sears, Brenda	F	9	1P	3	6	B
Resnick, Avi	M	10	2P	4	6	W
Shepard, Max	M	11	2P	5	6	W
Somers, Micah	M	9	2P	4	6	W
Stevens, Dierdre	F	10	2P	5	4	W
Stiles, Justin	M	9	2P	2	2	B
Stone, Adam	M	10	2P	3	2	B
Stouffer, Bruce	M	11	2P	3	5	W
Townsend, George	M	10	1P	1	3	B
Turnbull, Tania	F	10	1P	1	6	W
Turner, Dennis	M	11	JC	2	6	W

Name	Sex	Age	Household Structure	Household Income	Mother's Education	Race/ Eth.
Walker, Joanna	F	10	2P	1	4	W
Williams, Layla	F	11	1P	2	2	B
Wright, Jeffrey	M	12	2P	2	3	B

References

Achenbach, T., & Edelbrock, C. S. (1983). *Manual for the child behavior checklist and revised child behavior profile*. Burlington: Department of Psychiatry, University of Vermont.

Asher, S. R., Hymel, S., & Renshaw, P. D. (1984). Loneliness in children. *Child Development, 55*, 1456–1464.

Belle, D. (1982). Social ties and social support. In D. Belle (Ed.), *Lives in stress: Women and depression* (pp. 133–144). Beverly Hills: Sage.

Belle, D. (1989). Gender differences in children's social networks and supports. In D. Belle (Ed.), *Children's social networks and social supports* (pp. 173–188). New York: Wiley.

Belle, D., & Longfellow, C. (1983, April). *Emotional support and children's well-being: An exploratory study of children's confidants*. Paper presented at the biennial meeting of the Society for Research in Child Development, Detroit, MI.

Berman, B. D., Winkleby, M., Chesterman, E., & Boyce, W. T. (1992). After-school child care and self-esteem in school-age children. *Pediatrics, 89,* 654–659.

Bernard, J. (1981). The good provider role: Its rise and fall. *American Psychologist, 36*(1), 1–12.

Biller, H. B. (1976). The father and personality development: Paternal deprivation and sex-role development. In M. E. Lamb (Ed.), *The role of the father in child development.* New York: Wiley.

Blyth, D. A., & Foster-Clark, F. S. (1987). Gender differences in perceived intimacy with different members of adolescents' social networks. *Sex Roles, 17*(11/12), 689–718.

Bronfenbrenner, U. (1967, October 7). The split-level American family. *Saturday Review of Literature*, pp. 60–66.

Brown, J. S. T., Pratto, D. J., & Rodman, H. (1989). Social relationships as determinants of parental satisfaction with self-care arrangements for children. *Journal of Clinical Child Psychology, 18*, 8–15.

Bryant, B. (1985). The neighborhood walk: Sources of support in middle childhood. *Monographs of the Society for Research in Child Development, 50*, 3.

Bryant, B. (1989). The need for support in relation to the need for autonomy. In D. Belle (Ed.), *Children's social networks and social supports* (pp. 332–351). New York: Wiley.

Bryant, B. (1994). How does social support function in childhood? In F. Nestmann & K. Hurrelman (Eds.), *Social networks and social support in childhood and adolescence* (pp. 23–35). Berlin: Walter de Gruyter.

Bryant, B. K. (n.d.). *The child's perspective of sibling caretaking and its relevance to understanding social-emotional functioning and development.* Unpublished paper, University of California, Davis.

Cain, V. S., & Hofferth, S. L. (1989). Parental choice of self-care for school-age children. *Journal of Marriage and the Family, 51*, 65–77.

Caldwell, L. L., Smith, E. A., & Weissinger, E. (1992). Development of a leisure experience battery for adolescents: Parsimony, stability, and validity. *Journal of Leisure Research, 24*, 361–376.

Carnegie Corporation of New York. (1992). *A matter of time: Risk and opportunity in the nonschool hours.* New York: Author.

Caya, M. L., & Liem, J. H. (1998). The role of sibling support in high-conflict families. *American Journal of Orthopsychiatry, 68*(2), 327–333.

Coddington, R. D. (1984). Measuring the stressfulness of a child's environment. In J. H. Humphrey (Ed.), *Stress in childhood* (pp. 97–126). New York: AMS Press.

Cole, C., & Rodman, H. (1987). When school-age children care for themselves: Issues for family life educators and parents. *Family Relations, 36*, 92–96.

Colletta, N. (1979). Support systems after divorce: Incidence and impact. *Journal of Marriage and the Family, 41*, 837–846.

Commonwealth of Massachusetts Special Legislative Commission on Children in Need of Services. (1989). *The availability and affordability of programs for latch-key children.* A special report to the Great and General Court of Massachusetts, Boston.

Coontz, S. (1992). *The way we never were: American families and the nostalgia trap*. New York: Basic Books.

Coopersmith, S. (1967). *The antecedents of self-esteem.* San Francisco: Freeman.

Crnic, K., Greenberg, M., Ragozin, A., Robinson, N., & Basham, R. (1983). Effects of stress and social support on mothers of premature and full-term infants. *Child Development, 54*, 209–217.

Crockenberg, S. (1981). Infant irritability, mother responsiveness, and social support influences on the security of infant–mother attachment. *Child Development, 52*, 857–865.

Crouter, A. C., MacDermid, S. M., McHale, S. M., & Perry-Jenkins, M. (1990). Parental monitoring and perceptions of children's school performance and conduct in dual- and single-earner families. *Developmental Psychology, 26*, 649–657.

Crouter, A. C., McHale, S. M., & Bartko, W. T. (1993). Gender as an organizing feature in parent–child relationships. *Journal of Social Issues, 49* (3), 161–174.

Cutler, B. A., Smith, K. E., & Kilmon, C. (1995). Characteristics of fifth-grade children in relation to the type of after-school care. *Journal of Pediatric Health Care*, 167–171.

Diamond, J. M., Kataria, S., & Messer, S. C. (1989). Latchkey children: A pilot study investigating behavior and academic achievement. *Child and Youth Care Quarterly, 18*(2), 131–141.

Dwyer, K. M., Richardson, J. L., Danley, K. L., Hansen, W., Sussman, S., Brannon, B., Dent, C., Johnson, C. A., & Flay, B. (1990). Characteristics of eighth-grade students who initiate self-care in elementary and junior high school. *Pediatrics, 86*, 448–454.

Eccles, J., Midgley, C., Wigfield, A., Buchanan, C. M., Reuman, D., Flanagan, C., & MacIver, D. (1993). Development during adolescence: The impact of stage-environment fit on young adolescents' experiences in schools and in families. *American Psychologist, 48*(2), 90–101.

Edin, K., & Lein, L. (1997). *Making ends meet: How single mothers survive welfare and low-wage work.* New York: Russell Sage.

Elder, G. (1974). *Children of the Great Depression: Social change in life experience.* Chicago: University of Chicago.

Elder, G. H., Caspi, A., & Van Nguyen, T. (1986). Resourceful and vulnerable children: Family influence in hard times. In R. K. Silbereisen, K. Eyferth, & G. Rudinger (Eds.), *Development as action in context* (pp. 159–186). Berlin: Springer-Verlag.

Feiring, C., & Lewis, M. (1991). *How much do mothers know about their teenagers' social networks?: Implications for substance use.* Paper presented at the biennial meetings of the Society for Research in Child Development, Seattle, WA.

Finkelhor, D. (1979). *Sexually victimized children.* New York: The Free Press.

Fiske, M. (1982). Challenge and defeat: Stability and change in adulthood. In L. Goldberger & S. Breznitz (Eds.), *Handbook of stress: Theoretical and clinical aspects* (pp. 529–543). New York: The Free Press.

Floge, L. (1985). The dynamics of child-care use and some implications for women's employment. *Journal of Marriage and the Family, 47,* 143–154.

Folbre, N. and the Center for Popular Economics. (1995). *The new field guide to the U.S. economy.* New York: The New Press.

Fuchs, V. R. (1988). *Women's quest for economic equality.* Cambridge, MA: Harvard University Press.

Furman, W. (1989). The development of children's social networks. In D. Belle (Ed.), *Children's social networks and social supports* (pp. 151–172). New York: Wiley.

Furman, W., & Buhrmester, D. (1985). Children's perceptions of the personal relationships in their social networks. *Developmental Psychology, 21,* 1016–1022.

Furstenberg, F. F. (1994). History and current status of divorce in the United States. *The Future of Children, 4*(1), 29–43.

Galambos, N. L., & Garbarino, J. (1985). Adjustment of unsupervised children in a rural setting. *The Journal of Genetic Psychology, 146,* 227–231.

Galambos, N. L., & Maggs, J. L. (1991a). Children in self-care: Figures, facts, and fiction. In J. V. Lerner & N. L. Galambos (Eds.), *Employed mothers and their children* (pp. 131–157). New York: Garland.

Galambos, N. L., & Maggs, J. L. (1991b). Out-of-school care of young adolescents and self-reported behavior. *Developmental Psychology, 27*, 644–655.

Googins, B. K. (1991). *Work family conflicts: Private lives–public responses*. New York: Auburn House.

Gordon, L. (1994). *Pitied but not entitled: Single mothers and the history of welfare*. Cambridge, MA: Harvard University Press.

Guerney, L. F. (1991). A survey of self-supports and social supports of self-care children. *Elementary School Guidance and Counseling, 25*, 243–254.

Guisinger, S., & Blatt, S. J. (1994). Individuality and relatedness: Evolution of a fundamental dialectic. *American Psychologist, 49*, 104–111.

Hareven, T. (1989). Historical changes in children's networks in the family and community. In D. Belle (Ed.), *Children's social networks and social supports* (pp. 15–36). New York: Wiley.

Hawkins, A. J., & Crouter, A. C. (1991). Without map or compass: Finding the way in contemporary dual-earner marriages. In J. V. Lerner & N. L. Galambos (Eds.), *Employed mothers and their children* (pp. 211–235). New York: Garland.

Hetherington, E. M. (1989). Coping with family transitions: Winners, losers, and survivors. *Child Development, 60*, 1–14.

Hetherington, E. M., Cox, M., & Cox, R. (1982). Effects of divorce on parents and children. In M. Lamb (Ed.), *Nontraditional families* (pp. 223–285). Hillsdale, NJ: Lawrence Erlbaum Associates.

Hofferth, S. L., Brayfield, A., Deich, S., & Holcomb, P. (1991). *National child care survey, 1990*. Washington, DC: The Urban Institute.

Hoffman, L. (1979). Maternal employment. *American Psychologist, 34*, 859–865.

Howard, C. W., Broquet, A. J., & Farrell, A. D. (1991, April). *The impact of after-school context and supervision on urban middle school youth's prosocial and problem behaviors*. Paper presented at the biennial meeting of the Society for Research in Child Development, Seattle, WA.

Jeffers, C. (1967). *Living poor*. Ann Arbor, MI: Ann Arbor Publishers.

Jenkins, J. (1992). Sibling relationships in disharmonious homes: Potential difficulties and protective effects. In F. Boer & J. Dunn (Eds.), *Chil-*

dren's sibling relationships: Developmental and clinical issues (pp. 125–138). Hillsdale, NJ: Lawrence Erlbaum Associates.

Keller, S. (1963). The social world of the urban slum child: Some early findings. *American Journal of Orthopsychiatry, 33*, 823–831.

Kempton, T., Armistead, L., Wierson, M., & Forehand, R. (1991). Presence of a sibling as a potential buffer following parental divorce: An examination of young adolescents. *Journal of Clinical Child Psychology, 20*, 434–438.

Knight, D. (1997). Fear and loathing in suburbia. *Sanctuary: The Journal of the Massachusetts Audubon Society, 36*(5), 16–18.

Kon, I. S., & Losenkov, V. A. (1978). Friendship in adolescence: Values and behavior. *Journal of Marriage and the Family, 40*, 143–155.

Larson, R., & Richards, M. H. (1994). *Divergent realities: The emotional lives of mothers, fathers, and adolescents*. New York: Basic Books.

Long, T., & Long, L. (1982). *Latchkey children: The child's view of self care* (ERIC Document Reproduction Service No. ED 211 229).

Long, T., & Long, L. (1983). *Latchkey children* (ERIC Document Reproduction Service No. 226 836).

Longfellow, C., Zelkowitz, P. & Saunders, E. (1982). The quality of mother–child relations. In D. Belle (Ed.), *Lives in stress: Women and depression* (pp. 163–176). Beverly Hills: Sage.

Lovko, A. M., & Ullman, D. G. (1989). Research on the adjustment of latchkey children: Role of background/demographic and latchkey situation variables. *Journal of Clinical Child Psychology, 18*(1), 16–24.

Maccoby, E. (1984). Middle childhood in the context of the family. In W. A. Collins (Ed.), *Development during middle childhood: The years from six to twelve* (pp. 184–239). Washington, DC: National Academy.

Marshall, N. L., Coll, C. G., Marx, F., McCartney, K., Keefe, N., & Ruh, J. (1997). After-school time and children's behavioral adjustment. *Merrill-Palmer Quarterly, 43*, 497–514.

Martin, J. R. (1992). *The schoolhome: Rethinking schools for changing families*. Cambridge, MA: Harvard University Press.

McLoyd, V. (1993). Employment among African-American mothers in dual-earner families: Antecedents and consequences for family life and development. In J. Frankel (Ed.) *The employed mother and the family context* (pp. 180-226). New York: Springer.

Medrich, E., Roizen, J., Rubin, V., & Buckley, S. (1982). *The serious business of growing up: A study of children's lives outside school.* Berkeley: University of California Press.

Messer, S. C., Wuensch, K. L., & Diamond, J. M. (1989). Former latchkey children: Personality and academic correlates. *Journal of Genetic Psychology, 150*(3), 301–309.

Mulhall, P. F., Stone, D., & Stone, B. (1996). Home alone: Is it a risk factor for middle school youth and drug use? *Journal of Drug Education, 26*(1), 39–48.

National Study of Before- and After-School Programs. (1993). Final Report to the Office of Policy and Planning, U. S. Department of Education, Washington, DC.

Nightingale, C. H. (1993). *On the edge: A history of poor black children and their American dreams.* New York: Basic Books.

Nowicki, S., & Strickland, B. (1973). A locus of control scale for children. *Journal of Consulting and Clinical Psychology, 40*(1), 148–154.

Peterson, L. (1989). Latchkey children's preparation for self-care: Overestimated, underrehearsed, and unsafe. *Journal of Clinical Child Psychology, 18*(1), 36–43.

Pettit, G. S., Laird, R. D., Bates, J. E., & Dodge, K. A. (1997). Patterns of after-school care in middle childhood: Risk factors and developmental outcomes. *Merrill-Palmer Quarterly, 43*, 515–538.

Piotrkowski, C. (1978). *Work and the family system.* New York: The Free Press.

Posner, J. K., & Vandell, D. C. (1994). Low-income children's after-school care: Are there beneficial effects of after-school programs? *Child Development, 65*, 440–456.

Presser, H. B. (1986). Shift work among American women and child care. *Journal of Marriage and the Family, 48*, 551–563.

Quay, L. C. (1992). Personal and family effects on loneliness. *Journal of Applied Developmental Psychology, 13*, 97–110.

Richards, M. H., & Duckett, E. (1991). Maternal employment and adolescents. In J. V. Lerner & N. L. Galambos (Eds.), *Employed mothers and their children* (pp. 85–130). New York: Garland.

Richardson, J., Dwyer, K., McGuigan, K., Hansen, W., Dent, C., Johnson, C. A., Sussman, S., Brannon, B., & Flay, B. (1989). Substance use among eighth-grade students who take care of themselves after school. *Pediatrics, 84*, 556–566.

Richardson, J., Radziszewska, B., Dent, C. W., & Flay, B. R. (1993). Relationship between after-school care of adolescents and substance use, risk taking, depressed mood, and academic achievement. *Pediatrics, 92*(1), 32–38.

Riley, D. (1997). Using local research to change 100 communities for children and families. *American Psychologist, 52*(4), 424–433.

Riley, D., & Steinberg, J. (1993, March). *How should we define latchkey children? Contrasts of children in exclusive self-care, partial self-care, and sibling care*. Paper presented to the biennial meeting of the Society for Research in Child Development, New Orleans, LA.

Rodman, H., Pratto, D. J., & Nelson, R. S. (1985). Child care arrangements and children's functioning: A comparison of self-care and adult-care children. *Developmental Psychology, 21*, 413–418.

Rodman, H., Pratto, D. J., & Nelson, R. S. (1988). Toward a definition of self-care children: A commentary on Steinberg. *Developmental Psychology, 24*(2), 292–294.

Rosenthal, R., & Vandell, D. L. (1996). Quality of care at school-aged child-care programs: Regulatable features, observed experiences, child perspectives, and parent perspectives. *Child Development, 67*, 2434–2445.

Ross, J. G., Saavedra, P. J., Shur, G. H., Winters, F., & Felner, R. D. (1992). The effectiveness of an after-school program for primary grade latchkey students on precursors of substance abuse. *Journal of Community Psychology, 20*, 22–38.

Rutter, M. (1979). Protective factors in children's response to stress and disadvantage. In M. W. Kent & J. E. Rolf (Eds.), *Primary prevention of psychopathology: Vol. 3. Social competence in children*. Hanover, NH: University Press of New England.

Sampson, R. J. (1992). Family management and child development: Insights from social disorganization theory. In J. McCord (Ed.), *Facts, frameworks, and forecasts: Vol.3. Advances in criminological theory* (pp. 63–93). New Brunswick, NJ: Transaction Books.

Sandler, I. (1980). Social support resources, stress, and maladjustment of poor children. *American Journal of Community Psychology, 8*(1), 41–52.

Sandler, I., Miller, P., Short, J., & Wolchik, S. (1989). Social support as a protective factor for children in stress. In D. Belle (Ed.), *Children's social networks and social supports* (pp. 277-307). New York: Wiley.

Scarr, S. (1991). Foreword: Balancing work and family life: Why should it be so hard? In J. V. Lerner & N. L. Galambos (Eds.), *Employed mothers and their children* (pp. ix–xiv). New York: Garland.

Seligson, M. (1991). Models of school-age child care: A review of current research on implications for women and their children. *Women's Studies Int. Forum, 14*(6), 577–584.

Seligson, M., Fersh, E., Marshall, N. L., & Marx, F., with Baden, R. K. (1990). School-age child care: The challenge facing families. *Families in Society: The Journal of Contemporary Human Services, 71*, 324–331.

Seppanen, P. S., DeVries, D. K., & Seligson, M. (1993). *National study of before- and after-school programs: Executive summary*. Final report presented to the Office of Policy and Planning, U.S. Department of Education, Washington, DC.

Silverstein, B., & Krate, R. (1975). *Children of the dark ghetto*. New York: Praeger.

Stacey, J. (1991). *Brave new families: Stories of domestic upheaval in late twentieth century America*. New York: Basic Books.

Steinberg, J., & Riley, D. (1991, April). *Parents view self-care as a solution, not a problem*. Paper presented at the biennial meeting of the Society for Research in Child Development, Seattle, WA.

Steinberg, J., & Riley, D. (n.d.). *Parents' decisions about after-school care: The role of children's developmental press*. Unpublished manuscript, University of Wisconsin, Madison.

Steinberg, L. (1986). Latchkey children and susceptibility to peer pressure: An ecological analysis. *Developmental Psychology, 22*, 433–439.

Tietjen, A. M. (1982). The social networks of preadolescent children in Sweden. *International Journal of Behavioral Development, 5*, 111–130.

Tietjen, A. M. (1989). The ecology of children's social support networks. In D. Belle (Ed.), *Children's social networks and social supports* (pp. 37–69). New York: Wiley.

Todd, C. M., Albrecht, K. M., & Coleman, M. (1990). School-age child care: A continuum of options. *Journal of Home Economics, 32*, 46–52.

Toenniessen, C. S., Little, L. F., & Rosen, K. H. (1985). Anybody home?: Evaluation and intervention techniques with latchkey children. *Elementary School Guidance and Counselling, 12*, 105–113.

U. S. Department of Labor, Bureau of Labor Statistics. (1991). *Working women: A chartbook*. Washington, DC: U.S. Government Printing Office.

Vandell, D. L., & Corasaniti, M. A. (1988). The relation between third graders' after-school care and social, academic, and emotional functioning. *Child Development, 59*, 868–875

Vandell, D. L., & Ramanan, J. (1991). Children of the National Longitudinal Study of Youth: Choices in after-school care and child development. *Developmental Psychology, 27*, 637–643.

Vaux, A., Burda, P., & Stewart, D. (1986). Orientation toward utilization of support resources. *Journal of Community Psychology, 14*, 159–170.

Wahler, R. (1980). The insular mother: Her problems in parent–child treatment. *Journal of Applied Behavior Analysis, 13*, 207–219.

Wallerstein, J., & Kelly, J. (1980). *Surviving the breakup: How children and parents cope with divorce*. New York: Basic Books.

Weinraub, M., & Wolf, B. (1983). Effects of stress and social supports on mother-child interactions in single- and two-parent families. *Child Development, 54*, 1297–1311.

Weisner, T. (1989). Cultural and universal aspects of social support for children: Evidence from the Abaluyia of Kenya. In D. Belle (Ed.), *Children's social networks and social supports* (pp. 70–90). New York: Wiley.

Weisner, T., & Gallimore, R. (1977). My brother's keeper: Child and sibling caretaking. *Current Anthropology, 18*, 169–190.

Weiss, R. (1974). The provisions of social relationships. In Z. Rubin (Ed.), *Doing unto others* (pp. 17-26). Englewood Cliffs, NJ: Prentice Hall.

Weiss, R. (1979). Growing up a little faster: The experience of growing up in a single-parent household. *Journal of Social Issues, 35*, 97–111.

Weissman, M., & Paykel, E. (1974). *The depressed woman*. Chicago: University of Chicago Press.

Wenger, M. (1989). Work, play, and social relationships among children in a Giriama community. In D. Belle (Ed.), *Children's social networks and social supports* (pp. 91–115). New York: Wiley.

Werner, E., & Smith, R. (1982). *Vulnerable but invincible: A longitudinal study of resilient children and youth*. New York: McGraw-Hill.

Werner, E. E. (1990). Protective factors and individual resilience. In S. J. Meisels & J. P. Shonkoff (Eds.), *Handbook of early childhood intervention* (pp. 97–106). New York: Cambridge University Press.

Whiting, B., & Whiting, J. (1975). *Children of six cultures*. Cambridge, MA: Harvard University Press.

Whiting, B. B., & Edwards, C. P. (1988). *Children of different worlds: The formation of social behavior*. Cambridge, MA: Harvard University Press.

Williams, B. (1992). Poverty among African Americans in the urban United States. *Human Organization, 51*, 164–171.

Williams, C. (1991). *Black teenage mothers: Pregnancy and child rearing from their perspective*. Lexington, MA: Lexington Books.

Wolchik, S., Beals, J., & Sandler, I. (1989). Mapping children's support networks: Conceptual and methodological issues. In D. Belle (Ed.), *Children's social networks and social supports* (pp. 191-220). New York: Wiley.

Woodard, J. L., & Fine, M. A. (1991). Long-term effects of self-supervised and adult-supervised child care arrangements on personality traits, emotional adjustment, and cognitive development. *Journal of Applied Developmental Psychology, 12*, 73-85.

Woods, M. (1972). The unsupervised child of the working mother. *Developmental Psychology, 6,* 14–25.

Youcha, G. (1995). *Minding the children: Child care in America from colonial times to the present*. New York: Scribner.

Youniss, J. (1980). *Parents and peers in social development: A Sullivan–Piaget perspective*. Chicago: University of Chicago.

Youniss, J., & Smollar, J. (1985). *Adolescent relations with mothers, fathers, and friends*. Chicago: University of Chicago.

Zelizer, V. A. (1985). *Pricing the priceless child: The changing social value of children*. New York: Basic Books.

Zelkowitz, P. (1982a). *Children's support networks: Their role in families under stress*. Unpublished doctoral dissertation, Harvard Graduate School of Education, Cambridge, MA.

Zelkowitz, P. (1982b). Parenting philosophies and practices. In D. Belle (Ed.) *Lives in stress: Women and depression* (pp. 154–162). Beverly Hills: Sage.

Zelnik, M., & Kantner, J. F. (1977). Sexual and contraceptive experience of young unmarried women in the United States, 1976 and 1971. *Family Planning Perspectives, 9*, 55–71.

Zigler, E., & Finn-Stevenson, M. (1995). The child care crisis: Implications for the growth and development of the nation's children. *Journal of Social Issues, 51* (3) 215–231.

Zucker, H. L. (1944). Working parents and latchkey children. *Annals of the American Academy of Political and Social Science, 236*, 43–50.

Index

A

B

C

D

G

H

I

J

K

N

O

P

T

U

V

W

Y

Z